A Family Guide to Joy
(in All Circumstances)

Travis L. Zimmerman

Editors: Annie Schreiber, Ph.D; Lance Clark
Front cover design and artwork: Treyton D. Zimmerman
Back cover design and interior layout: Matthew J. Elliott
Proofreader: Gail Eckenroad

Library of Congress Cataloging In-Publication Data
Zimmerman, Travis L., 1969 December 26
A Family Guide to Joy (in All Circumstances)/ Travis L. Zimmerman

Includes biographical references.
ISBN-10: 1721781455
ISBN-13: 978-1721781454

First Printing: July 2018

A Family Guide to Joy
(in All Circumstances)

To Jesus, the greatest joy of my life

TABLE OF CONTENTS

HOW DO I USE THIS GUIDE?

You can benefit several ways from *A Family Guide to Joy*.

Individuals – This guide is a quick read about how we can know joy by following Jesus through all of our trials. In fact, with *A Family Guide to Joy*, you'll look at your trials in a whole new way!

Family Time – From kids to parents, *A Family Guide to Joy* is an excellent blend of Biblical references and personal challenges and triumphs. This guide's transparent approach delivers a joyful and educational message that will grow your family closer to Christ.

Small Group Bible Studies – Whether you're a group leader, a Sunday School teacher, or a small group participant, *A Family Guide to Joy* will benefit your group. This guide serves as a multi-week study with chapter-ending questions that encourage not only group interaction and discussion but also personal reflection and growth.

Challenge-seekers – Why not take what you've learned and put it into action? The end of each chapter has a unique challenge — 12 in all — to encourage you to practically apply what you've learned from Jesus. Discover the challenges that await you!

UP FOR A CHALLENGE?

The Joy Challenges

I commit this day to taking on The Joy Challenges:

1. What are you willing to sacrifice to know joy in your life?

2. Explain how you can know joy in good times.

3. Describe how you can know joy in your daily work.

4. Articulate how you can know joy in transitions.

5. Consider how you can know joy through your most broken relationship.

6. Reflect on how you can know joy in the death of a loved one.

7. Discover how you can know joy in rejection.

8. Share how you can know joy in pain.

9. Talk about how you can know joy in sickness.

10. Expand on how you can know joy by crying out in misery.

11. Choose one way you can die to self and how you'll go about it.

12. How can *you* know joy in all circumstances? Share your answer with a friend.

_____   _____
Signature   Date

TAKE THE JOY CHALLENGES!

With your new guide, bring your family and friends together for a fun, small group study and work through The Joy Challenges to know joy in all circumstances!

- FREE on App Store and Google Play (search name: JOY!)

- Easy to use

- Great for individuals, families, and small groups

- Experience joy in a completely new way!

FOREWORD

I've known Travis for over ten years and, in that time, we have walked through a number of life's challenges. In all those potentially transformational moments, Travis has maintained a joy in his heart that has not only seen him through but has brought comfort and hope to those around him.

His enthusiastic love for Jesus is evident no matter when or where you find him. In *A Family Guide to Joy* you will find a carefully guided way to discover that joy for yourself.

Travis answers difficult questions and gives insightful direction from the Bible he loves and the experiences God has walked him through.

Whether you read this alone or with a study group or with your family you, will be encouraged to walk with a joy that is infectious and life-changing.

Pastor Dave Biser
Harrisburg, PA

INTRODUCTION

A DESPERATE CRY...

Swollen tears streamed down my face, ignoring my best efforts to disguise them. No use.

"How could they do that to Him?" I whispered to the darkness engulfing me.

The tears flowed faster now, even as my nose filled up too. From my throat came a pathetic whimper, prompting my wife Suzanne to ask, "Travis, are you OK?"

I wasn't, not at all. How could they *do* that to Him?

The year was 2004, and Suzanne and I were taking in our first viewing of Mel Gibson's *The Passion of the Christ*. By this point in the story, we as an audience had:

- witnessed Jesus' mock trial before the Sanhedrin,
- winced at Pilate's cowardice in the face of Jewish opposition, and
- gasped over the savage beatings Jesus endured at the hands of the Roman soldiers.

The film now focused on Jesus as He staggered up the Via Dolorosa ("Way of Suffering"). He stumbled from pain, exhaustion, and blood loss on His way to the cross.

Gibson's focus shifted to Jesus' mother Mary. She struggled to push her way through Jerusalem's crowded streets to catch a glimpse of her condemned Son. Jesus collapsed again as Mary pushed forward, desperate to reach Him. All the while, Roman soldiers beat Jesus with whips and hurled insults at Him.

Again, I asked incredulously, "How could they do that to Him?!"

Mary turned the corner just in time to see Jesus crumble again beneath the cross' weight. Horror marred her face as she witnessed her beloved Son fall to the earth. And during one of the film's tenderest moments, a flashback showed when Jesus was just a little boy. In this scene, young Jesus stumbled downstairs as an alarmed Mary was unable to catch His fall. This mirrored what she would witness years later on the Via Dolorosa, except that in the flashback she coddled her boy in her arms, comforting and caring for Him. Flash forward and the implication is clear: Mary was able to comfort Him then, but she could *not* comfort Him now.

And I lost it. LOST IT!

I am not exaggerating when I say I cried for 20 minutes; I could not stop! Embarrassed looks came not only from my wife but also from many of the people around us. "Hold yourself together, man!" they seemed to silently scream.

How could they DO that to Him?!

The movie concluded soon after that, Jesus victoriously ascending from the grave. And then God threw the switch on me, turning mourning to joy! In reliving Jesus rising from the grave, such joy filled my heart, a joy I hadn't previously experienced, even on Easter Sundays. God changed my perspective: my tears of sadness turned to tears of joy!

As the lights came up in the theatre, I still couldn't compose myself, and crumpled tissues fell from my hands. The shocked audience exited in reflective silence. And I had a reflection of my own. I didn't know from where it came, but in my heart, I silently, desperately cried out: **Jesus, I just want to _know_ You!**

Although I had known Jesus as my Lord and Savior since I was eight, I now sensed I was crying out to know Him in a deeper way than before. I wasn't asking for cattle on a thousand hills, or superior intellect, or a greater social position. In fact, I didn't know exactly what I was asking for, only that it was the most desperate cry of my heart: to _know_ Jesus more closely.

Little did I know then how God would answer my heart's most desperate cry beyond any measure or expectation! He did this by working through my life's greatest celebrations and bitterest tragedies. Fourteen years later, His answer still overwhelms me with utter joy!

This guide describes how God answered that desperate cry. In doing so, it also addresses a question we've all asked ourselves, but whose answer continues to elude us: How can I know joy in all circumstances?

God's answer will both surprise and challenge you!

PART 1

LAYING THE FOUNDATION

"We don't feel deeply or strongly enough. It would seem that Our Lord finds our desires not too strong, but too weak. We are half-hearted creatures, fooling about with drink and sex and ambition when infinite joy is offered us, like an ignorant child who wants to go on making mud pies in a slum because he cannot imagine what is meant by the offer of a holiday at the sea. We are far too easily pleased."
~ C.S. Lewis, *The Weight of Glory, and Other Addresses*

Jesus' Journey to Joy®

Chapter 1

Jesus knew joy because He modeled joy.
(Matthew 11:28-30)

1

THE REASON FOR JOY

Consider it pure joy, my brothers and sisters, whenever you face trials of many kinds, because you know that the testing of your faith produces perseverance.
James 1:2-3 (NIV)

"Come to me, all you who are weary and burdened, and I will give you rest. Take my yoke upon you and learn from me, for I am gentle and humble in heart, and you will find rest for your souls. For my yoke is easy and my burden is light."
Matthew 11:28-30 (NIV)

There is joy in serving Jesus,
as I journey on my way,
joy that fills the heart with praises,
every hour and every day.
~ Oswald J. Smith

> ### Jesus knew joy because He modeled joy.

This is a story about a journey to joy. Well, three stories actually, but I'll get to that soon enough.

And while you would naturally expect a book called joy to *define* joy, it might surprise you to see that this book also discusses how God *brings about* joy.

We all experience our share of good times and bad times — often concurrently. How great it would be to know joy through every station of life's journey! That leads me to the key question this guide seeks to answer.

> ## Key Question:
> How can I know joy in all circumstances?

How we answer that question plays a big part in how we look at life. To know joy not in a few circumstances, not in most circumstances, but in ALL circumstances – regardless of what happens to us – is certainly worth considering.

So if joy is important to us, let's take some time to consider just what joy means.

Joy is...

Joy is the simplest form of gratitude.
> ~ Karl Barth

The *Evangelical Dictionary of Theology* defines joy as:

> a delight in life that runs deeper than pain or pleasure. From a Biblical perspective it is not limited by nor solely tied to external circumstances. Joy is a gift of God, and like all of his other inner gifts it can be experienced even in the midst of extremely difficult circumstances.

That's a good working definition for us. Jesus is all about joy!

Joy is... knowing Jesus

Now this is eternal life, that they may know You, the only true God, and Jesus Christ, whom You have sent.
> John 17:3 (BSB)

The apostle John, the disciple whom Jesus loved, put to words so well my desperate cry of 2004: Jesus, I just want to *know* You. It's this guide's main premise.

> **Premise:** Joy is knowing Jesus, following Him through all our trials.

It's a partnership: we don't walk alone; and we walk with Jesus in good times and bad, all for His glory!

Joy is…learning from Jesus

"Come to me, all you who are weary and burdened, and I will give you rest. Take my yoke upon you and learn from me, for I am gentle and humble in heart, and you will find rest for your souls. For my yoke is easy and my burden is light." Matthew 11:28-30 (NIV)

The yoke that Jesus mentions in Matthew 11:28-30 emphasizes the challenges and responsibilities of partnering with Christ through our lives. In analyzing these verses, the *NIV Life Application Study Bible* describes it this way.

> Jesus doesn't offer a life of luxurious ease – the yoke is still an oxen's tool for working hard. But it's a shared yoke, with the weight falling on bigger shoulders than yours. Someone with more pulling power is up front helping. Suddenly you are a participant in life's responsibilities with a great Partner – and now that frown can turn into a smile, and that gripe into a song.

In essence, Jesus teaches us how to turn our burdens into joy. At heart, Jesus is a teacher (John 13:13), the best one ever. Whether Jesus privately huddled with His disciples or publicly instructed the masses, He took the time to explain to His audiences the Father's ways. Now these are available to us through God's Word. Jesus taught many lessons during His lifetime. The timing on <u>understanding</u> these lessons happens in three ways:

1. **Understanding can come immediately**. After the apostles were flogged, they immediately understood one of Jesus' lessons. Acts 5:41 (NLT) says, "The apostles left the high council rejoicing that God had counted them worthy to suffer disgrace for the name of Jesus." Pain notwithstanding, most of us want to immediately learn the lessons Jesus teaches us. At least we think we do!

2. **Understanding can come later**. While washing His disciples' feet, Jesus taught, "You do not realize now what I am doing, but later you will understand" (John 13:7 NIV). It may be days, years, or even

decades later that the Holy Spirit brings understanding of what He taught us earlier. The dog show disaster I share in chapter 7, Joy in Rejection, took place 30 years before I learned the lessons from it.

3. **Understanding may not come in this life.** As the martyrs of Revelation 6:10 (BSB) cry out, "How long, O Lord, holy and true, until You judge those who live on the earth and avenge our blood?" Martyrs or not, our desire to understand why God does what He does seems just as urgent. In these instances and for various reasons, God in His sovereignty will often shield us from understanding. We have to trust Him to work all things together for His glory and our good (Romans 8:28). After all, He's God, and we're not!

Whatever the timing of our understanding, this guide celebrates the eternal joy we have in Jesus, as well as the joy God brings through the lessons He teaches in the midst of all kinds of circumstances. These lessons show:

- How God moves through circumstances;
- How He uses all things for His good; and
- How we grow in Christ as a result of our trials, sufferings, and challenges.

Many of these lessons are among the most impactful of our lives: talk about joy! Jesus is the reason for joy, and the lessons we learn from His teaching are as priceless as they are joyful!

Joy is...taking up our cross and following Jesus daily

Then he said to them all, "If anyone wants to follow after me, let him deny himself, take up his cross daily, and follow me."
Luke 9:23 (CSB)

The lessons Jesus teaches us come at a price: taking up our cross daily and following Him. Jesus talked the talk and walked the walk. Taking up our cross is something we can do right now, today. It's not an academic exercise to ponder but a faith walk to travel together with Him.

Joy is...in God's Word

Many Scripture passages, including the following three, reinforce this definition of joy:

- A fruit of the Spirit (Galatians 5:22)

- The hope of the righteous (Proverbs 10:28)

- Trials of many kinds (James 1:2)

We'll focus on James's characterization of pure joy. Facing trials of many kinds isn't something we would readily associate with pure joy. Yet it is a central concept in God's Word, and therefore one of this guide's key verses.

> **Key Verse:** Consider it pure joy, my brothers and sisters, whenever you face trials of many kinds, because you know that the testing of your faith produces perseverance. James 1:2-3 (NIV)

As an engineer, I see a formula for pure joy in James 1:2-3. It looks something like this:

Pure joy = trials of many kinds = testing of your faith → perseverance

Put another way, pure joy is progressing through all types of trials, which leads to perseverance. I may not like the progression, but I do like the result. Being mature and complete, not lacking anything is goal-worthy, but are we willing to go through trials of many kinds to reach that result?

The fact is: we can't really choose to *not* go through trouble! Jesus said so in John 16:33 (NIV): "I have told you these things, so that in me you may have peace. In this world you will have trouble. But take heart! I have overcome the world."

And how about those trials?

A Word on Trials

Though we may not like to admit it, many of us — both new and longtime believers — hold a skewed outlook on what it means to follow Christ in the midst of trials. But when we recall the joy we experienced in giving our life to Him, we can more easily identify with the perspective Johnny Nash shows in his joyous tune, "I Can See Clearly Now":

I can see clearly now, the rain is gone,
I can see all obstacles in my way
Gone are the dark clouds that had me blind
It's gonna be a bright (bright), bright (bright) Sun-Shiny day.

No doubt! It's gonna be a bright (bright), bright (bright) Sun-Shiny day…until it's not! Even after giving our life to Christ, something goes wrong with our bright Sun-Shiny day, as the once gone clouds now reappear! We lose our hair, we lose our wallet, we lose our job, we lose a loved one and, suddenly, it seems, we lose our way! Then we yell out to God, "Why are you doing this to me?! It's supposed to be a bright Sun-Shiny day! Where are all these trials coming from and when will they end (so I can get back to my bright Sun-Shiny life)?"

In commenting on Jacob's joys and struggles with God, his family, and his extended family, the *NIV Life Application Study Bible* describes this tendency well of how God blessed him in the midst of his trials.

> Many people believe that Christianity should offer a problem-free life. Consequently, as life gets tough, they draw back disappointed. Instead, they should determine to prevail with God through life's storms. Problems and difficulties are painful but inevitable; you might as well see them as opportunities for growth. You can't prevail with God unless you have troubles to prevail over.

Again, this is just what Jesus promised: in this world you will have trouble. After all, we live in a fallen world. So, rather than trials just being something that we have to "put up with" to get to the joy we want, not unlike having to eat your broccoli to get to your ice cream dessert, it's just the opposite. Not only are trials intertwined with our lives, they are intertwined with our joy as well! In Philippians 4:4, one of my favorite Scripture passages, the apostle Paul rings out, "Rejoice in the Lord always!"

Dr. R.C. Sproul enlightens:

> How is it possible to remain joyful all the time? Paul gives us the key: "Rejoice *in the Lord always*" (emphasis added). The key to the Christian's joy is its source, which is the Lord. If Christ is in me and I am in Him, that relationship is not a sometimes experience. The Christian is always in the Lord and the Lord is always in the Christian, and that is always a reason for joy. Even if the Christian cannot rejoice in his circumstances, if he finds himself passing through pain, sorrow, or grief, he still can rejoice in Christ. We rejoice in the Lord, and since He never leaves us or forsakes us, we can rejoice always.

Knowing this, we've got to address the proverbial "elephant in the room", the simultaneous emotions that often accompany trials.

Is it Joy vs. Happiness? Or is it bittersweet?

In my background research for this guide, I quickly found passionate discussions about whether joy and happiness are synonyms and whether joy is permanent while happiness is temporary. Well-respected theologians, whose names you'd recognize, hold differing opinions; but solving that disagreement isn't central to this guide's focus. What is critical to understand, however, is how we can have two opposite emotions simultaneously. Here are two personal examples.

- When my daughter Elizabeth graduated from high school and prepared for college, I felt a mix of emotions: I wept tears of joy over her accomplishments but tears of sadness over her soon leaving the house. My emotions were bittersweet.

- When my dad died from dementia complications, I was relieved that he no longer suffered and joyous that Jesus welcomed him home, but I was also deeply saddened to lose my father at age 63. Again, my emotions were bittersweet.

In my view, what sometimes gets lost in the discussion of joy vs. happiness is that when we go through life's joys and trials, we often grapple with different emotions — joy and sadness. We generally don't just experience one emotion. Neither Jesus nor James is suggesting we're going to be joyful when a loved one dies, a child grows up and moves away, or we lose a job. That would be both ludicrous and unbiblical: God created us with feelings! Yet I can have joy all the time, because I have Jesus all the time and in all circumstances! Still, we'll also experience a bittersweet range of emotions that God will work through for His glory and our good.

Now, as I previewed earlier, this is a story of joy; three stories actually.

The Three Stories of Joy

"Didn't the Messiah have to suffer these things and enter into His glory?"
        Luke 24:26 (HCSB)

Of course, our first story is about Jesus.

Jesus' Journey to Joy

Let us fix our eyes on Jesus, the pioneer and perfecter of our faith, who for the joy set before Him endured the cross, scorning its shame, and sat down at the right hand of the throne of God.
        Hebrews 12:2 (NIV)

Jesus knew joy, because He modeled joy.

Jesus, fully God and fully man, experienced the full range of human experiences and emotions throughout His earthly ministry. Jesus knew that He was born to die to fulfill God's plan to rescue man from his sin, according to the will of our God and Father (Galatians 1:4). The author of Hebrews exhorts us to take encouragement from Jesus, "who for the joy set before Him endured the cross, scorning its shame and sat down at the right hand of the throne of God" (Hebrews 12:2).

In other words, the crux of Jesus' Journey to Joy was the cross: His life before it, His death upon it, and His resurrection from it! Jesus modeled His life on earth in His journey to and from the cross. From that bedrock, this guide highlights milestones from Jesus' public ministry. And it is a journey we can walk with Him (see Jesus' Journey to Joy at the beginning of this chapter).

Jesus' Journey to Joy establishes a framework for our own faith journey with Christ by considering our joys and sorrows in light of His. Highlights MacDonald, "As the saintly Scot, Robert Murray McCheyne said, for every look we take at ourselves we should take ten looks at Christ."

My Journey to Joy

In the 15 years between 2004 and 2018, our family experienced an intense period of testing that we've nicknamed our Time of Trials. But God has delivered us from them all! During our Time of Trials we experienced:

- Deaths of 3 of our 4 parents

- Five near-suicides

- The loss of my wife's health for 6 years due to a horrific accident

- Over a half million dollars in medical bills

- Three job losses

- Two near-bankruptcies due to the loss of our life's savings

- The near-loss of our marriage

- Dozens of lost friends due to our prolonged situation

- Hundreds of doctors' appointments and ER visits

- Over a dozen surgeries

Note: My Journey to Joy is not a primer on the range of joys and trials we humans go through. I've never lost a wife or a child, I've never experienced twins, I've never been divorced, and I've never climbed a famous mountain range. None of my five kids has walked away from the Lord, none has ever played college sports, and I've never suffered constant pain. Yet several of my friends have experienced each of these joys and trials.

I point this out because our joys and trials should never be a source of pride for us — only a source of joy in the Lord. Whether we suffer more or less than someone else is not ours to judge: none but our God knows our heart, how much suffering we can take, and what our capacity to endure is at any point. So through this guide, we will draw lessons primarily from Jesus' experiences, but also secondarily from my own personal trials.

In fact, the experiences of our joy and suffering are a lot like an RV Motorhome Exterior State Sticker Map of the US (see image). People add states to their maps as they reach new destinations, but you'll rarely see one map that's fully complete. So it is with life's experiences: we won't experience every situation ("state"), but we will experience enough of them to understand the joys and pains of others. This is a humbling thought.

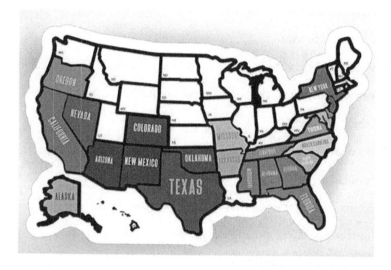

Regardless of how full our "sticker map" is, God works through our joys and trials powerfully, often subtly, but always unmistakably. Again, you will marvel at the lessons He imparts through our lives, because you will see God's faithfulness to us, especially in times of trials.

One reason I wrote this book was to encourage you in your Journey to Joy. Again, this guide's premise is that our joy is in knowing Jesus and following Him through all our trials. You've already started out on your journey long ago: you've got a lot of "state stickers." Here are four aspects of this guide that will encourage you on your Journey to Joy:

1. You'll be inspired by Jesus' Journey to Joy.
2. You'll learn lessons — 113 in all — from these trials and challenges that you can apply to your life.
3. You'll talk and think through targeted questions — 83 in all — about your own Journey to Joy.
4. You'll be issued a challenge at the end of each chapter — 12 in all — that will grow your faith.

With that said, let's kick off your Journey to Joy.

Your Journey to Joy

JOY CHALLENGE #1: What are you willing to sacrifice to know joy in your life?

CHAPTER 1 QUESTIONS:

1.   What are you looking to get out of this study?
2.   What are you looking to contribute to this study?
3.   In your own words, how would you define joy?
4.   What's stealing your joy right now?
5.   How did Jesus model joy?
6.   How does knowing Jesus help us walk joyfully in our faith?

Jesus' Journey to Joy®

Chapter 2

Jesus knew joy because He celebrated in good times.
(John 2:1-2)

2

JOY IN GOOD TIMES

On the third day there was a wedding at Cana of Galilee, and the mother of Jesus was there; and both Jesus and His disciples were invited to the wedding.
        John 2:1-2 (AMP)

Zip-a-dee-doo-dah, zip-a-dee-ay,
My, oh, my, what a wonderful day,
Plenty of sunshine headin' my way;
Zip-a-dee-doo-dah, zip-a-dee-ay!
        ~ Ray Gilbert

> ## Jesus knew joy because He celebrated in good times.

Celebrations are a wonderful aspect of God's kingdom

In John chapter 2 we learn that Jesus, His family, and His disciples were invited to a wedding at Cana of Galilee. Bible Study Tools notes the several stages in a Jewish wedding culminated in a feast, a time of great celebration. These feasts were grand affairs that could last for as many as seven days.

At this particular wedding in Cana of Galilee, Jesus performed His first recorded miracle: turning water into wine, and a fine wine at that. Though Jesus' miracle was quietly done, the master of the feast understood the depth of the act, exclaiming, "'Everyone brings out the choice wine first and then the cheaper wine after the guests have had too much to drink; but you have saved the best till now.' What Jesus did here in Cana of Galilee was the first of the signs through which he revealed his glory; and his disciples believed in him" John 2:10-11 (NIV).

The immediate joy was over the fine wine, but the lasting joy is that His disciples put their hope in Christ.

Whether Jesus turned water into wine (John 2:10-11), or multiplied five loaves and two fish into a feast for five thousand men, besides women and children (Matthew 14:13-21), or healed a blind man (John 9:25), a clear lesson emerges.

> ## Lesson learned #1:
> Jesus knew joy because He celebrated in good times!

Since most of us desire to have joy, we should consider where true joy originates.

Joy in Creation

In the beginning of God's Word and creation, we learn that He created the heavens and the earth. Each day God commented on His creation:

- The first day: God created the heavens and the earth and spoke light in existence. And God saw that the light was good. (Genesis 1:4)

- The second day: God created the sky. (Genesis 1:8)

- The third day: God created the land and saw that it was good. (Genesis 1:12)

- The fourth day: God created the stars and heavenly bodies and declared them good. (Genesis 1:18)

- The fifth day: God created water life and birds, and He declared them good. (Genesis 1:21)

- The sixth day: God created all creatures living on dry land and declared them good (Genesis 1:25). But when He created man and female in His own image, He responded with an even greater joy:

"And God saw everything that he had made, and behold, it was very good." (Genesis 1:31 NLT)

Gill's exposition of Genesis 1:31 discusses God's supreme pleasure in creating man and woman:

> And behold, it was very good; it had been said of everything else, at the close of each day's work, excepting the second, that it was good; but here the expression is stronger upon the creation of man, the chief and principal work of God, that it was "very good"; he being made upright and holy, bearing the image of his Creator upon him, and in such circumstances as to be happy and comfortable himself, and to glorify God.

We have inherent purpose, intrinsic value, and built-in happiness, because God created us in His image!

Lesson learned #2:
God created us in joy. We are "very good" because we are made in His image!

Joy originates from God. So how did He visibly manifest that joy during Jesus' earthly ministry?

Joy demonstrated

In one of the Bible's greatest celebrations, a demurring John the Baptist baptized Jesus in the Jordan River. Here, for God's glory, the Father, the Son, and the Spirit were present to all assembled witnesses. Matthew celebrated in 3:16-17 (CEV), "So Jesus was baptized. And as soon as he came out of the water, the sky opened, and he saw the Spirit of God coming down on him like a dove. Then a voice from heaven said, 'This is my own dear Son, and I am pleased with him.'"

What a celebration that must have been! We can imagine the sun pouring down upon God's creation as He opened the heavens. But that would be nothing in comparison to God's radiance. The writer of 1 Chronicles celebrates God's glorious majesty in 16:27 (ESV): "Splendor and majesty are before him; strength and joy are in his place."

In the final chapter of the book of Revelation, with Christ reigning and evil banished forever, John rejoices in the New Jerusalem: "The city [that] has no need for the sun, neither of the moon, to shine, for the very glory of God illuminated it, and its lamp is the Lamb" (Revelation 21:23 WEB). Our God is the source of all light — and of all joy!

Lesson learned #3:
God is the manifestation of our joy.

Want to see Jesus joyous?

Jesus was a man of the people who interacted with all ages. Yet I've always been particularly enamored over His love for the children who flocked to Him. As a dad of five kids, I receive such joy from my children. How much more joy does Jesus receive from each child He created! The image of Jesus laughing with children seated on His lap and encircling Him is sublime. It seems He took that same joy into many of His parables.

Jesus celebrated not only in His personal life but also in the many public parables that "went over the heads" of the Pharisees. He delighted the masses who so often adored Him. To me, Luke 15 highlights the joy Jesus experienced through celebrations of finding something once lost.

- The Parable of the Lost Sheep – "Suppose one of you has a hundred sheep and loses one of them. Doesn't he leave the ninety-nine in the open country and go after the lost sheep until he finds it? And when he finds it, he **joyfully** puts it on his shoulders and goes home. Then he calls his friends and neighbors together and says, **'Rejoice with me**; I have found my lost sheep.' I tell you that in the same way there will be more **rejoicing in heaven** over one sinner who repents than over ninety-nine righteous persons who do not need to repent." Luke 15:4-7 (NIV)

- The Parable of the Lost Coin – "Or if there is a woman who has ten silver coins, if she should lose one, won't she take a lamp and sweep and search the house from top to bottom until she finds it? And when she has found it, she calls her friends and neighbours together. **'Come and celebrate with me'**, she says, **'for I have found that coin I lost.'** I tell you, it is the same in Heaven — there is **rejoicing among the angels of God** over one sinner whose heart is changed." Luke 15:8-10 (PHILLIPS)

- The Parable of the Lost Son – "Then his son said to him, 'Father, I've sinned against heaven and you. I don't deserve to be called your son anymore.' The father said to his servants, 'Hurry! Bring out the best robe and put it on him. Put a ring on his finger and sandals on his feet. Bring the fattened calf, kill it, and **let's celebrate with a feast.** My son was dead and has come back to life. He was lost but has been found.' **Then they began to celebrate.**" Luke 15:21-24 (NOG)

Within this short chapter, Luke recounts Jesus talking about joy, rejoicing, feasting, and celebrating! And here's where God showed me a lesson that I'm thrilled to share with you now. Not only is each of these a parable of celebration, but they all focus on sinners repenting of their old ways and claiming new life in Christ. The beautiful lesson is simply this.

Lesson learned #4:

Jesus is most joyous when we turn from death to life: it's a heavenly celebration!

My Journey to Joy

I'm thankful to celebrate a life lived in joy for Christ!

The dream life

The best times of my life are probably much like the best times of your life, too.

- Taking Jesus as my Lord and Savior.

- Marrying my best friend, Suzanne.

- Celebrating the birth of each of our five children.

- Rejoicing in each of our kids coming to faith in Christ.

- Sharing love and laughter with our family and friends.

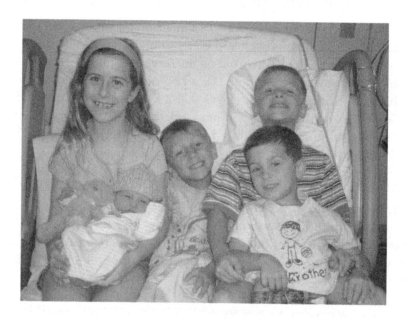

We all have these amazing moments, milestones to look back upon. And they are wonderful to celebrate! But, at the end of each ordinary day, as I lay my head on my pillow, I try to thank God for at least one wonderful thing He did that day. These moments might include:

- My kids succeeding in their schoolwork.

- A buddy getting a new job he wanted.

- God answering a long-time prayer request.

- The beautiful constellation I enjoyed just before bedtime.

- My back being less sore today than it was yesterday.

These little joys are no less celebratory than the best times of my life, because God is in them all. And after I made a habit of celebrating that fact for several years, God brought me to a breathtaking conclusion, another lesson learned in joy.

Lesson learned #5:
God is the author of the best times of our lives!

After all, Jesus is the Author of Life (Acts 3:15), the Author and Perfecter of our faith (Hebrews 12:2), and the Author of our salvation (Hebrews 2:10)!

With all these good times, big and small, you might think I'm crazy for even asking this next question.

Can a good time be a trial?

What a question! Like me, maybe you haven't given this much thought before. But let me offer three answers to the question.

Answer #1: Yes! When *all* we're expecting out of life are good times, we develop unrealistic expectations. King Solomon notes in Ecclesiastes 7:14 (NIV), "When times are good, be happy; but when times are bad, consider this: God has made the one as well as the other."

Good times are great, but bad times are part of our journey, too. And, bad times (often known as "trials") are where God grows our perseverance.

Lesson learned #6:
Be careful of letting good times become a trial by relying on them too heavily as your source of joy.

Answer #2: Yes, because our hearts can become proud, and we will forget the Lord our God. Moses cautioned the second generation of Israelites, as they prepared to cross over into the Promised Land, not to forget God:

> When you eat and are full, you will praise the LORD your God for the good land He has given you. Be careful that you don't forget the LORD your God by failing to keep His command — the ordinances and statutes — I am giving you today. When you eat and are full, and build beautiful houses to live in, and your herds and flocks grow large, and your silver and gold multiply, and everything else you have increases, be careful that your heart doesn't become proud and you forget the LORD your God who brought you out of the land of Egypt, out of the place of slavery. (Deuteronomy 8:10-14 HCSB)

Moses saw first-hand how easily the Israelites forgot God, whether that was when they built a golden calf or when they grumbled about the food they were eating or water they were drinking.

Lesson learned #7:

Success can turn your good times into bad times. Don't forget God.

Answer #3: Yes, because we'll be tempted to think we produced the good times. Moses continued to caution the Israelites not to fall into the trap of self-reliance.

> He led you through the big desert that brought fear with its poisonous snakes and scorpions and thirsty ground where there was no water. He brought you water out of hard rock. In the desert He fed you bread from heaven, which your fathers did not know about. He did this so you would not have pride and that He might test you. It was for your good in the end. Be careful not to say in your heart, 'My power and strong hand have made me rich.' (Deuteronomy 8:15-17 NLV)

Moses previously spoke of pride's danger, and here he warns that pride can bring us to the point where we feel we don't need God anymore. That arrogance is repugnant to God. Especially today, we can hold those same arrogant beliefs of self-reliance.

> ### Lesson learned #8:
> So that your celebration in joy continues, give credit to Whom credit is due.

Or else…

Moses warns about what happens if we forget God and become prideful:

> You must remember the LORD your God, for he is the one who gives ability to get wealth; if you do this he will confirm his covenant that he made by oath to your ancestors, even as he has to this day. Now if you forget the LORD your God at all and follow other gods, worshiping and prostrating yourselves before them, I testify to you today that you will surely be annihilated. Just like the nations the LORD is about to destroy from your sight, so he will do to you because you would not obey him. (Deuteronomy 8:18-20 NET)

Sobering. God's Word certainly makes a convincing case that good times can indeed be a trial.

> ### Lesson learned #9:
> Good times without God are not good times at all.

I'll conclude our discussion of joy in good times with a delightful question.

What's your best moment ever?

Now that we've savored the good times in the dream life, I'm going to ask you the question I've asked literally thousands of people.
 Of all the joys, celebrations, and transitions God's taken you through in your life, what's your best moment ever?

Earlier I shared some of my life's best moments. Now it's your turn. What's your best moment ever?

* The Christmas you got your first bike?

* The moment your brother or sister was born?

* The state championship your high school team won?

Think about it: what was your best moment *ever*? Perhaps it's the time you'd go back to revisit if God allowed you. Or it's that time you repeatedly savor in your mind and which gets sweeter as you age. Maybe you have a couple of them, but most of us have at least one best moment ever.

Take a moment right now to picture it in your mind....

To get you thinking, rejoice with me as I share some of the answers I've received to this question over the years.

* "My best moment ever," shared a mom seated next to her husband, "occurred right after the birth of our second son. It began tragically: his umbilical cord was wrapped around his neck, so he came out blue because he couldn't breathe. It was all a blur, but we could tell from the rising voices that things weren't going well. Finally, they resuscitated him, and he took his first breath of air. We praised God together!" Her husband burst into tears of joy as his wife concluded the story. Actually, we all did.

* A longtime alcoholic nearly lost his family and his life, spending years "on and off the wagon" of recovery. Finally, he turned to Christ for help. He shared, "My best moment ever happened when my adult daughter — who I had hurt so badly over the years — finally began

returning my affection when she saw my recovery was real, grounded in Christ. She bought two kayaks for us, because it was something we had enjoyed doing together when she was little. She wants to rebuild our relationship by starting from the beginning." He also burst into tears, thanking God for restoration.

- "My best moment," one young man publicly shared, "was when God brought me out of my heroin addiction. I spent my youth in rebellion, getting kicked out of school, and lots of trouble with the law. After a few bad overdoses I finally hit rock bottom. But Jesus was waiting there for me, and He brought me out. It hasn't been easy — still isn't — but my worst moment became my best moment because of Jesus."

Whether your best moment springs from joy or tragedy, again, this is the time you'd go back to if you could. That time of absolute joy.

Still imagining it? Still thinking back? How does it feel?

Now, consider this: **Your time with Jesus in heaven will be a zillion times better than your life's best moment here on earth!**

That's not to say that we're to be "so heavenly focused that we're not any earthly good" — no! God has us here for a reason: to serve Him and others, to bring Him glory, and to help in carrying out His perfect plan. Yes, our time on earth can be both glorious and trial-filled, but we must never forget Whom we serve and the joy we will have in bringing glory to His name! Truly, a picture of heaven is a picture of serving Jesus fully! That will be collectively our best moment ever — serving Jesus for all eternity!

Lesson learned #10:

Your time with Jesus in heaven will be a zillion times better than your life's best moment on earth!

This guide is all about building that relationship with Jesus to know true joy. Again, joy is knowing Jesus, and following Him through all our trials.

<u>Your Journey to Joy</u>

JOY CHALLENGE #2: Explain how you can know joy in good times.

CHAPTER 2 QUESTIONS:

1. Knowing that God is the source of all joy, how does this change your outlook?
2. Why does Jesus seem most joyous when we turn from death to life?
3. Which lesson was most helpful to you? Why?
4. How can a good time become a trial?
5. Why are good times without God not good times at all?
6. What's your life's best moment? Why?

PART 2

JOY THROUGH OUTER TRIALS

"Oh, life is like that. Sometimes, at the height of our revelries, when our joy is at its zenith, when all is most right with the world, the most unthinkable disasters descend upon us."
~ Ralphie as an adult, A Christmas Story, MGM, 1983.

Jesus' Journey to Joy®

Chapter 3
Jesus knew joy because He provided through His daily works. (John 4:34)

3

JOY IN DAILY WORK

"My food," said Jesus, "is to do the will of him who sent me and to finish his work." John 4:34 (NIV)

O, how full of briers is this working-day world.
~ William Shakespeare, As You Like It

> # Jesus knew joy because He provided through His daily work.

Then, like now, the majority of a person's day consisted of working for a living. In other words, working was a major component of Jesus' Journey to Joy: Jesus provided.

Jesus in the work-a-day world

Like His earthly father Joseph, Jesus was a carpenter.

- "Isn't this the carpenter's son?" Matthew 13:55 (WEB)
- "Isn't this the carpenter?" Mark 6:3 (GWT)

Jesus was a hard worker who provided for His family. Can you imagine eating at a table He made? Because employment is something most of us can relate to, many of Jesus' parables include work and lessons learned from it. All have this lesson in common: we serve the Lord through our work.

> ### Lesson learned #11:
> Even the Son of Man provided for his family. Colossians 3:23-24 reminds us that we work for the Lord, and as a reward, receive an inheritance from Him. We are serving the Lord Christ.

Regarding that inheritance, Isaiah 61:7 (ISV) promises a beautiful blessing: "Instead of your shame you will receive double, and instead of disgrace people will shout with joy over your inheritance; therefore you will inherit a double portion in their land; everlasting joy will be yours."

Talk about joy in employment!

Work of supreme importance

But Jesus worked for much more than His family's financial provision. His biggest job? Check this out.

> Therefore, when Christ came into the world, he said:
> "Sacrifice and offering you did not desire,
> but a body you prepared for me;
> with burnt offerings and sin offerings
> you were not pleased.
> Then I said, 'Here I am — it is written about me in the scroll
> — I have come to do your will, my God.'"
> Hebrews 10:5-7 (NIV)

Jesus came to do His Father's will. And this is our biggest job, too!

> ### Lesson learned #12:
> God isn't looking for your sacrifice and offerings: He's looking at your heart and your obedience to Him. When we open ourselves up to do the will of God, our work will be the best we've done.

Work can be frustrating

I've often wondered what it would have been like to work in the Garden of Eden *before* the Fall, when conditions were perfect – literally. Growing up, I pulled weeds, swatted gnats, and endured humidity to help my family get a decent harvest from our backyard garden. It could be frustrating but also rewarding. I often wanted to give up. In His work, Jesus also faced frustrations with His co-workers' (read "disciples") lack of belief.

- Then Jesus said to them, "Don't you understand this parable? How then will you understand any parable?" Mark 4:13 (NIV)

- "Are you still so dull?" Jesus asked them. Matthew 15:16 (NIV)

Each time I read these above passages, I get the distinct sense Jesus could have been talking about me! At times, my unbelief seems to eclipse faith. But don't worry: His grace far exceeds His frustration.

Lesson learned #13:
Our unbelief affects our work and can often be frustrating to God, but He doesn't give up on us.

And many powerful people opposed His work

Jesus' earthly work threatened the status quo and the world's powerful people, who feared His teaching would diminish their power and position.

> Again he entered the synagogue, and a man was there who had a withered hand. They watched him to see whether he would cure him on the Sabbath, so that they might accuse him. And he said to the man who had the withered hand, "Come forward." Then he said to them, "Is it lawful to do good or to do harm on the Sabbath, to save life or to kill?" But they were silent. He looked around at them with anger; he was grieved at their

hardness of heart and said to the man, "Stretch out your hand." He stretched it out, and his hand was restored. The Pharisees went out and immediately conspired with the Herodians against him, how to destroy him. Mark 3:1-6 (NRSV)

Lesson learned #14:

We will always have work frustrations, but they are trials God uses to grow our patience, pride, and perseverance. Stick with it on your way to becoming mature and complete, not lacking anything.

Jesus balanced work and time with His Father

Why does it often seem that when things get really busy at work, the first thing to go are our quiet times with God? It's kind of like turning your headlights *off* before entering a long tunnel! But it was never that way with Jesus: He knew how to balance His work time and quiet time. Jesus knew the joy of communing with His Father, especially through His "quiet times."

- Very early the next morning before daylight, Jesus got up and went to a place where he could be alone and pray. Mark 1:35 (CEV)
- Yet he often withdrew to deserted places and prayed. Luke 5:16 (CSB)

The more time we spend alone with God, the more attuned we are to His Word, His will, and His work. I find that when I shortcut this part of my day, I feel disconnected, more easily agitated, and often unproductive. In short, my choice to skip that time with my Father robs me of my joy.

Lesson learned #15:

Jesus made time for His Father, and so should we. Spending time with our Father can be among the most joy-filled moments of our day. It's like a replenishing energy boost drink except totally pure!

And in the end, He came to do His Father's work

Jesus had a job to do, and He knew it. And it's a team effort.

> My food, said Jesus, is to do the will of him who sent me and to finish his work. Don't you have a saying, "It's still four months until harvest"? I tell you, open your eyes and look at the fields! They are ripe for harvest. Even now the one who reaps draws a wage and harvests a crop for eternal life, so that the sower and the reaper may be glad together. Thus the saying "One sows and another reaps" is true. I sent you to reap what you have not worked for. Others have done the hard work, and you have reaped the benefits of their labor." John 4:34-38 (NIV)

Evangelical Convictions highlights that God's gospel is accomplished through the work of Christ. And most of all through His work on the cross (we'll talk about this in more detail in Part 4: Victorious Joy!).

Lesson learned #16:

The Father's work is a team approach, led by Jesus. Make no mistake: Jesus' work on the cross is sufficient – we can do nothing to add to or subtract from it. But join Him here in the joyous kingdom work He has for us!

Jesus provided salvation

If we get right down to it, God sent His Son Jesus to the world. Jesus' job? To provide salvation, as Jesus declares in John 3:16-17 (ESV): "For God so loved the world, that he gave his only Son, that whoever believes in him should not perish but have eternal life. For God did not send his Son into the world to condemn the world, but in order that the world might be saved through him."

Lesson learned #17:
Jesus' work is to save the world, and this is the most important work of all. We can join Him in His work now just by asking Him!

Jesus had the perfect job, right? Sometimes we seem to have a "perfect" job, too. Sometimes we don't.

My Journey to Joy

A great job: joining God in His glorious work

So I decided there is nothing better than to enjoy food and drink and to find satisfaction in work. Then I realized that these pleasures are from the hand of God. Ecclesiastes 2:24 (NLT)

One of the best jobs I ever had was when I was just 5 years old: doing carpentry work with my dad.

My dad worked days as a forester, but nights and weekends he often delighted in carpentry projects around the house. He produced all kinds of amazing work: renovated bedrooms, wooden decorations for Mom, even a greenhouse for her flowers. Dad liked to work alone, but as a five-year-old, I got up the courage to ask, "Daddy, can I help you build something?"

Taking a break from his carpentry work, Dad glanced down at me and nodded his head, "Sure, Big T."

I was elated! Would I get to saw the wood? Swing a hammer? Maybe even use the power saw? My imagination thrilled at the possibilities awaiting me. But Dad had a completely different job in mind.

Holding the nail.

No matter. When my turn came to hold the nail, turns out I was holding it the wrong way! "Son," Dad patiently explained, "you want to hold the nail straight up and down, not sideways or tilted. It will bend like that. Here, hold it like this."

His hands dwarfed my matchstick fingers to hold the nail true. After some practice, I could hold several nails in place while Dad pounded them home. The sense of accomplishment — even at the age of five — was overwhelming. I felt like Mr. Big Pants!

<u>Lesson learned #18:</u>
Sometimes insignificant jobs can be the best jobs!

Did Dad *need* me to hold the nails for him in his work? No! But did Dad *allow* me to hold the nail for him? YES! And that relates to a spiritual truth about working on our journey to joy.

The thought of joining God in His work is thrilling, but it can be a little intimidating (as we see, for example, when Moses was intimidated about being God's spokesman in Exodus 4:10). Whether you're an electrician, an architect, or a ministry volunteer, your work is important to God. But sometimes we overestimate just *how* important that godly work actually is. At one point in my adult career, I was so fulfilled in doing His work that I began to think, "Hey, God *needs* me to do this work for Him!"

And that's where I learned a big lesson: God doesn't *need* me to do anything. Anything! Shocked?

I'm not an English major like my daughter, but the verb 'need' in relation to God is critical. God is sovereign unto Himself: there's nothing we can add or take away from Him. So, if God truly *needed* me to accomplish something, there's one thing I can guarantee you: sooner or later, I will let Him down.

In other words, God wouldn't be sovereign (of course, He is!) if He needed me to do something, since I'm going to fail, just like you would. Here's the distinction — and the joy: God *allows* us to join Him in His work! Dad didn't *need* me to hold the nail, he *allowed* me to hold the nail.

> ## Lesson learned #19:
> God doesn't need us to do His work, but He allows us to join Him in His work. Rejoice in His work through you!

Lunch atop a Skyscraper (Branded Entertainment Network)

"Meh" jobs

May the God of hope fill you with all joy and peace in believing, so that by the power of the Holy Spirit you may abound in hope. Romans 15:13 (ESV)

Let's be real: sometimes the job you're doing isn't as cool as holding nails for your dad. Then again, it isn't a totally miserable job either (our next section). Dozens of my buddies, and many others, are currently in "meh" jobs. And in my Journey to Joy, I've been there plenty of times. It seems these "meh" jobs:

- Pay the bills,

- Have decent benefits, and

- Remind us of The Righteous Brothers' song, "You've lost that loving feeling…!"

Many of us would say, "Hey, don't complain, at least you have work!" That's true, but we should be honest about our attitude towards jobs. And we need to stay open to how God can help us know joy in a "meh" job. Here are the next five lessons God's taught me on my Journey to Joy in a "meh" job.

Five lessons learned in knowing joy in a "meh" job:

Lesson Learned #20:

Cursed from the Garden. Because Adam sinned, God said, "cursed is the ground for your sake; in sorrow shall you eat of it all the days of your life" (Genesis 3:17 AKJV). Though our work will be hard, God will provide through it. Go all in!

Lesson Learned #21:

Take the long view. King David rejoiced in Psalm 16:5-6 (HCSB), "Lord, You are my portion and my cup of blessing; You hold my future. The boundary lines have fallen for me in pleasant places; indeed, I have a beautiful inheritance." The same God holds our future, too, and the long view looks very bright.

Lesson Learned #22:

Relate to people not by griping, but by persevering. Do everything without complaining…" (Philippians 2:14 BSB). Face it: most of us have worked jobs we're not thrilled with, but complaining brings us (and others) down. Allow God to mold your testimony in Him, so that you can help others. Remember, joy is knowing Jesus, following (persevering with) Him through all our trials.

Lesson Learned #23:

Pursue God in your work, and He will flourish you. King Solomon knew much about flourishing: "So I decided there is nothing better than to enjoy food and drink and to find satisfaction in work. Then I realized that these pleasures are from the hand of God" (Ecclesiastes 2:24 NLT). Flourishing doesn't necessarily mean more money, but certainly more peace.

Lesson Leaned #24:

Make money your goal, and you invite misery. The apostle Paul cautions, "For the love of money is a root of all kinds of evil" (1 Timothy 6:10 NKJV). Remember, money isn't evil, but loving money can pierce you with many griefs.

Remembering that God works through our "meh" jobs helps us persevere. But sometimes a "meh" job becomes a miserable job.

Miserable jobs

So they took Jeremiah and put him into the cistern of Malkijah, the king's son, which was in the courtyard of the guard. They lowered Jeremiah by ropes into the cistern; it had no water in it, only mud, and Jeremiah sank down into the mud.

Jeremiah 38:6 (NIV)

I'll keep this section short, but we can't ignore it: sometimes we're stuck in a miserable job. Sometimes, like Jeremiah, we sink down into the mud. This is nothing new: miserable jobs date back to Biblical times.

- **Being exploited**: Jacob complained to his exploitive boss Uncle Laban, "I was consumed by heat during the day, consumed by frost during the night, and my sleep fled from my eyes. This is how it's been for me twenty years in your house. I served you fourteen years for your two daughters, and six years for your flocks — and you changed my salary ten times!" (Genesis 31:40-41 TLV).

- **Getting pinned to the wall**: As a member of King Saul's court and an object of his jealousy, David almost lost his life early: "Saul tried to pin him to the wall with his spear, but David eluded him as Saul drove the spear into the wall." (1 Samuel 19:10 NIV).

- **Sinking down into the mud**: In trying to warn the Israelites to repent or face God's judgment, Jeremiah was *literally* stuck in the mud of a miserable job (Jeremiah 38:6).

Today, although much has changed professionally, much remains the same. One cynical man told his kids, "Get a job that makes a ton of money. You're going to end up hating it anyway, so you might as well be wealthy in your misery."

Frankly, that's terrible advice. Hopefully this is better advice. I've been in a few miserable jobs, and here are the next five lessons God taught me on my journey through them:

Five lessons learned in knowing joy in a miserable job:

Lesson Learned #25:

A bad boss helps you know a good boss. I get it: you don't click with your boss. Whether it's favoritism, politics, or double standards, God can teach you much through a bad boss: patience, increased prayer, perseverance. The upside? Having a bad boss will help you better appreciate a good boss when you do get one.

Lesson Learned #26:

A miserable job helps you recognize a good job. Downsizing, transitions in leadership, and mergers all have the potential to make jobs miserable. But miserable jobs can happen without any of those factors. No job is completely miserable (well, there was that one time…). God will help you recognize a good job when it arrives.

Lesson Learned #27:

Patience, please. In one miserable military job where I begged God to give me patience, a co-worker near retirement chided me, "Lieutenant Zimmerman, do you think there's a better chance that God will simply give you patience, or that He will put you in situations to grow your patience?" I shut up.

Lesson Learned #28:

A time of transition. People stuck in miserable jobs often speak of "being in the wrong seat on the bus" or even "being on the wrong bus." These are true statements. In my 25 years of the work-a-day world, I've seen people struggle like fish on a bicycle, and I've been one of them. The waiting can drive you crazy. But lean on Jesus during your time of transition, because leaning on Him brings joy! He is your comfort.

Lesson Learned #29:

No, really, it's a time of transition. And, then, sometimes God has a time of unemployment for you, but that's the topic of our next chapter.

Your Journey to Joy

JOY CHALLENGE #3: Describe how you can know joy in your daily work.

CHAPTER 3 QUESTIONS

1. Why is our work of supreme importance to God?
2. How well do you balance your work time and your quiet times with God? How can you improve this?
3. What's the greatest job you've had? Most miserable job you've had? Why?
4. How did God bring joy through these jobs?
5. Which lesson was most helpful to you? Why?
6. List three things God is teaching you in your daily work.

Psalms of Joy

O come, let us sing joyfully to the LORD;
Let us shout joyfully to the rock of our salvation.

Let us come before His presence with a song of thanksgiving;
Let us shout joyfully to Him with songs.

For the LORD *is a great God*
And a great King above all gods,

In whose hand are the depths of the earth;
The peaks of the mountains are His also.

The sea is His, for He made it, by His command;
And His hands formed the dry land.

Psalm 95:1-5 AMP

Jesus' Journey to Joy®

Chapter 4

Jesus knew joy because He prayed in transitions.
(Luke 22:41-42)

4

JOY IN TRANSITIONS

He withdrew about a stone's throw beyond them, knelt down and prayed, "Father, if you are willing, take this cup from me; yet not my will, but yours be done."
Luke 22:41-42 (NIV)

It's a recession when your neighbor loses his job; it's a depression when you lose yours.
~ President Harry S. Truman

Jesus knew joy because He prayed in transitions.

Transitions galore

Transitions come in many forms: life, home, relationships, and jobs. Because of its broad applicability and inherent challenges, I'm going to focus this section on transition from a job: unemployment.

Now, to be clear, Jesus Himself was never unemployed. However, He did transition from His earthly ministry to being raised from the dead and then seated at the Father's right hand. And that transition, though infinitely more difficult than our own employment transitions, teaches us about how to know joy in our own trials.

First hints

Among the first hints of Jesus' pending transition occurred right after Peter's confession of the Christ. About a year before His death and resurrection, Jesus warned His disciples that His earthly work was ending. His masterstroke — His work on the cross — loomed ahead of Him. Matthew foreshadowed, "From that time on Jesus began to show His disciples that He must go to Jerusalem and suffer many things at the hands of the elders, chief priests, and scribes, and that He must be killed and on the third day be raised to life" (16:21 BSB).

The gospel narratives then chronicle Jesus' inexorable walk *to* the cross for His imminent work *on* the cross.

Lesson learned #30:
Our transitions on earth — employed or unemployed — should be regarded in light of the cross. Jesus modeled transitions for us.

Jesus is goal-oriented

When it comes to accomplishing goals, corporate presidents and chief financial officers have nothing on Jesus. Jesus knew what the Father had called Him to do, and He was undeterred in carrying out those plans through His transition. Although the Pharisees warned Jesus to flee because Herod wanted to kill Him, Jesus responded with undeterred resolve in Luke 13:32 (NIV): "Go tell that fox, 'I will keep on driving out demons and healing people today and tomorrow, and on the third day I will reach my goal.'"

Of course, Jesus is speaking here of His atoning sacrifice for our sins (1 John 2:2) and His resurrection on the third day. This supreme goal necessitated a remarkable transition from Jesus' earthly ministry to heaven in three steps.

1. He descended to the dead;
2. On the third day He rose again;
3. He ascended into heaven!

> ### Lesson learned #31:
> Jesus' goal was the cross and dying for humanity's sin, and reaching that goal required major transitions. God can use our transitions — including unemployment — to accomplish His and our goals.

No holding back

His transition looming, Jesus continued His work unabated for the Father's glory, even as He revealed that the prince of this world (Satan) would play a part in that transition. In the Upper Room, Jesus instructed His disciples on what was to come.

> You heard me say, "I am going away and I am coming back to you." If you loved me, you would be glad that I am going to the Father, for the Father is greater than I. I have told you now before it happens, so that when it does happen you will believe. I will not say much more to you, for the prince of this world is coming. He has no hold over me, but he comes so that the world may learn that I love the Father and do exactly what my Father has commanded me. Come now; let us leave.
> John 14:28-31 (NIV)

> ### Lesson learned #32:
> If Satan has no hold on Jesus, he also has no permanent hold on us, either. You will continue to experience God's presence in any transition.

In heaven, Jesus' permanent priesthood continues, for He "always lives to intercede for [those who draw near to God through Him]" (Hebrews 7:25 BSB).

This brings us to the key action Jesus modeled through His employment transition: Jesus prayed both publicly and privately.

Jesus prayed publicly

As Jesus and His disciples concluded the Passover feast, the Last Supper, He publicly prayed His "high priestly prayer." Here Jesus prayed to be glorified, prayed for His disciples, and prayed for all believers. In this short but powerful prayer to the Father, Jesus affirmed His transition: "I brought glory to you here on earth by completing the work you gave me to do" (John 17:4 (NLT).

His work was nearly finished, but there was still a long hill to climb before the transition

---

Lesson learned #33:

With Jesus' "high priestly prayer" as our guide, our public prayers during our own transitions can bless others.

Jesus prayed privately

Jesus then journeyed to the Mount of Olives, accompanied by His inner circle of Peter, James, and John. Knowing what lay ahead, Jesus told His disciples to pray. Luke records in 22:39-40 (TPT), "Jesus left the upper room with his disciples and, as was his habit, went to the Mount of Olives, *his place of secret prayer.* There he told the apostles, 'Keep praying for strength to be spared from the severe test of your faith that is about to come.'"

Jesus knew that praying — talking with God — would protect both His disciples and Himself. God's rescue plan of sending His Son to the cross surely weighed heavily on Jesus' heart. We hear that concern in Jesus' Gethsemane prayers.

> He withdrew about a stone's throw beyond them, knelt down and prayed, "Father, if you are willing, take this cup from me; yet not my will, but yours be done." An angel from heaven appeared to him and strengthened him. And being in anguish, he prayed more earnestly, and his sweat was like drops of blood falling to the ground. Luke 22:41-44 (NIV)

Here we appreciate the dual nature of Christ — fully God and fully man. As fully God, Jesus knew what the Father was commanding Him to do. As fully man, Jesus anticipated the physical and spiritual pain of crucifixion. Jesus knew that His death and rebirth were the only way to save humankind. Despite His agony, He repeatedly asked the Father for help to persevere through to completion.

> ### Lesson learned #34:
> With Jesus' Garden of Gethsemane prayer as our guide, our private prayers during our own transitions help us persevere to do the Father's will.

Go time!

When the hour of transition came, Jesus met it head on. Matthew recounts in 25:45-46 (NLT), "Then he came to the disciples and said, 'Go ahead and sleep. Have your rest. But look — the time has come. The Son of Man is betrayed into the hands of sinners. Up, let's be going. Look, my betrayer is here!'"

When He finished praying, Jesus bravely faced His own transition. Jesus purposed to obey the Father, knowing full well what pain lay ahead of Him. He approached it with boldness and strong leadership because He anticipated His final transition from the earth would be His most important work of all. Jesus' "best" work lay ahead of Him.

> ### Lesson learned #35:
> Just as Jesus' best work lay ahead of Him, so your best work may lay ahead of you! So when "Go time!" comes for your transition, embrace the opportunity to go where God leads you.

Wait patiently for the Lord

Not everyone will experience the joys of employment transitions. Yet each of us will experience transitions of some kind: family, friends, work. From my vantage point, I can wholeheartedly affirm that God, through my own times of unemployment, has indeed used those transitions to bring me closer to Him.

God did this to put me on the path to my best work yet: obeying and serving Him to a greater degree each day. What a joy! Unemployment certainly isn't something any of us aspires to "achieve", but it's another life situation that God will use to accomplish His perfect plan for your life. That leads to a key lesson.

Lesson learned #36:

Naturally speaking, most of us plan for employment. However, that may not be God's plan for us at certain times of our lives. Accepting that God has temporarily sidelined us for His purposes teaches us to wait patiently for the Lord.

Here are some of the ways God used my times of unemployment to teach me perseverance in my Journey to Joy.

My Journey to Joy

I wish I could say that you get used to it, but you don't. Well, not any more than you get used to getting your thumb slammed in a car door.

Unemployment.

Men's Health reports that out of all suicide deaths worldwide, researchers estimate that 1 in 5 are tied to unemployment, or an estimated 45,000 suicides each year. Little wonder, since losing a job means not just losing income, but often our self-esteem, too. I should know: I was unemployed three (almost five) times within six years.

More velocity

Six months into my information technology sales job, cracks began to emerge. Concerned about my sales performance, the company president, whom I'll call Don, flew in for a day to accompany me on a blitz of sales calls. After two joint calls, it became clear that our sales philosophies didn't line up: I prioritized honesty, while Don prioritized getting the sale regardless of the means.

Forty-eight hours later, I received a call from Don and his chief financial officer. At first I desperately tried to engage them in small talk. But suddenly, with the subtlety of a dump truck driving through a nitroglycerin plant, the president cut me off mid-sentence. "Travis, we've looked at what you bring to the company and where we're headed. I've decided to terminate your employment with us."

Ouch! I felt the proverbial punch to my solar plexus.

Don continued, "I can tell that you're a good sales guy, and I know there's a company that's going to be lucky to get you. But we're trying to really get up to speed here, and I need someone with more velocity to attack the territory."

Um, that's Dilbert-speak for, "You don't measure up."

The icing on the cake came as the CFO mumbled something about me receiving a small severance package if I promised not to sue the company for wrongful termination.

But now came the hardest part: sharing this little employment update with Suzanne. Stumbling out of my home office to find her, I prayed, asking God to protect our family. My throat tightened as I saw her.

"Suzanne, I just lost my job."

Turning pale, she meekly asked, "What are we going to do, Travis?"

"I really don't know, but God does," I said quietly. "He will guide us through this."

Lesson learned #37:
Even in the midst of turmoil, God gave us such peace to wait on Him.

Grocery Store Show-off

Now I had spare time, so Suzanne often sent me grocery shopping to get me out of the house. My strategy was to shop on weekdays, to avoid all my friends who worked day jobs. As men, they'd no doubt ask, "Hey, buddy, where are you working at these days?"

No matter how I answered that, it would confirm what people were probably thinking anyway: "That Travis, I *knew* he was a no-good, do-nothing loser!"

Then one morning I spotted my buddy "Jason" at the end of the aisle I had just wheeled my cart into. Too late! Jason called out my name, almost embarrassingly loudly.

"Hey, Jason!" I timidly greeted him. And before I could brace myself, he said, "Hey, Travis, what are you doing these days?"

Oh, no! My cover was blown! Luckily my sales training kicked in, and I turned Jason's question back on him: "Hey, Jason, what are YOU doing these days?"

Jason's response went something like this.

"Well, Travis, things have been going kinda well for my family. I was humbled to be awarded employee of the decade, second time in a row. My wife's research project received presidential funding due to the ground-breaking work she's been accomplishing at the lab. My oldest is studying abroad as a Rhodes Scholar, my middle son's team just won states, and my youngest is trying to decide between Harvard or M.I.T. The big question, though, is where to vacation this year: Southern France or Tuscany?"

Suddenly he glanced at his watch and said, "Oh, I've got to jet! Awesome to see you, Travis!" And he whisked off, leaving me in my deepening depression.

Whew – that was a CLOSE one! I almost had to reveal what a total loser I was!

Lesson learned #38:

God used unemployment to highlight a recurring sin: my pride. And God will also use your greatest weaknesses to teach you humility.

But it got worse! At the checkout counter the cashier announced the total and asked how I'd like to pay. I decided to use my PA Access Card (translation: food stamps). Normally I would have taken my Access Card out of my wallet, but today, with people behind me, I left the card in my wallet and furtively flashed it to the cashier.

"Sir," the cashier rolled her eyes, "I can't see what you're showing me for payment." Can't see it?! The card is BLAZE YELLOW!

I felt my face flush with humiliation. The cashier sighed, "You're going to have to take that Access Card out so I can see it." I dared not turn to see the people's expressions. My eyes glued to the floor, I packed up, tail between my legs, and headed for home.

During those lean times, God taught me the wisdom of Paul's words to the Philippians: "I know what it is to be poor or to have plenty, and I have lived under all kinds of conditions. I know what it means to be full or to be hungry, to have too much or too little" (4:12 CEV).

Lesson learned #39:

In unemployment, God helped me better understand that the secret of being content in any situation is to totally rely on Him.

Flashback: Who are these people?

Several months earlier, I had applied for state assistance. Even though I was the breadwinner in our house with a stay-at-home mom and five young kids, I was still surprised to learn that we might qualify for food stamps. Humbling.

After the county assistance office lost my application and didn't return my calls, I knew I had to go in-person to the county office. The long lines soured my mood. "Didn't I get my educational degrees to *avoid* experiences like this?" I mumbled to myself.

The man ahead of me was talking to an officer about his parole. Behind me a mother tried to quiet her kids and complained about their daddies owing money. Under my breath, I said, "God, you are SO testing me! I shouldn't be here! Who ARE these people?"

> **And immediately, God shot back at me, "Travis, YOU are these people!"**

Busted! God admonished me that I was no better or worse than anyone in this line, or anyone on this earth. In my desire to avoid uncomfortable situations like unemployment and food stamps, I had placed myself above people who made less money. So I prayed:

"Please forgive me, Lord, for elevating myself above others. We are all Your people. If these unemployment experiences are meant to humble me, then Lord, humble me."

Lesson learned #40:

God corrects our ugly attitudes, humbling us for work in His kingdom. God helped me understand that the ground is level at the foot of the cross. Freed of my professional hubris, I now saw that Jesus had my back, and He knew I was unemployed.

Now it's time to think through your transitions.

Your Journey to Joy

JOY CHALLENGE #4: Articulate how you can know joy in transitions.

CHAPTER 4 QUESTIONS:

1. Our transitions on earth — employed or unemployed — are in light of the cross. Jesus modeled transitions for us. How so?
2. Jesus prayed through His transition. How can prayer help us through our transitions?
3. Which lesson was most helpful to you? Why?
4. Why does unemployment carry such a stigma even though so many have been unemployed?
5. Does unemployment indicate failure or success? Why?
6. How can you minister to someone who's in transition right now?

Jesus' Journey to Joy®

Chapter 5

Jesus knew joy because He forgave in relationships.
(Luke 23:34)

5

JOY IN RELATIONSHIPS

Jesus said, "Father, forgive them, for they do not know what they are doing."
Luke 23:34 (NIV) (Jesus' first statement from the cross)

Intense love does not measure, it just gives.
~ Mother Teresa

Jesus knew joy because He forgave in relationships.

For the next seven chapters, we'll track the seven actions Jesus demonstrated and which correspond with His last seven sayings on the cross. As we track Jesus' Journey to Joy on the following pages, you'll see all seven points on the cross. The cross was the greatest podium of all time! Imagine the view Jesus had of His audience for the words He spoke (James 1:9). Despite the horrid situation, Jesus had the joy of seeing whom He was saving and why He was saving them.

> ### Lesson learned #41:
> The cross was the greatest podium of all time! Christ ascended this relic designed to deliver death, transforming it into a stage to declare life for all.

As Jesus journeyed towards the joy set before Him (Hebrews 12:2), His relationships were among His greatest joys and greatest trials. Although both friends and enemies let Him down, we see Jesus consistently modeling a powerful response for us: He forgave.

Unforgiveness snuffs out joy. Worse, it's a sin. Jesus commands in Matthew 6:14-15 (ERV), "Yes, if you forgive others for the wrongs they do to you, then your Father in heaven will also forgive your wrongs. But if you don't forgive others, then your Father in heaven will not forgive the wrongs you do."

Let's see how Jesus reaped joy by demonstrating forgiveness in His relationships.

Jesus forgave His enemies

Jesus prepared His followers by demonstrating the attitude they should take toward their enemies. In Matthew 5:11-12 (NET) He says, "Blessed are you when people insult you and persecute you and say all kinds of evil things about you falsely on account of me. Rejoice and be glad because your reward is great in heaven, for they persecuted the prophets before you in the same way."

Lesson learned #42:
Rejoice and be glad because great is your reward in heaven.

And the prophets before us suffered but also received their reward.

Lesson learned #43:
You are not alone in your suffering at the hands of your enemies.

However, Jesus didn't play the doormat or cower before His enemies. Instead, He boldly confronted them in their sin, especially the Jewish leaders in their hypocritical ways: "But woe to you, scribes and Pharisees, hypocrites, because you shut off the kingdom of heaven from people;

for you do not enter in yourselves, nor do you allow those who are entering to go in" (Matthew 23:13 NASB).

Jesus boldly calling out these hypocritical leaders led to predictable results, which John sadly noted in 11:53 (WNT): "So from that day forward they planned and schemed in order to put Him to death."

> ### Lesson learned #44:
> Be ready to challenge authorities if they're in the wrong. This may bring additional trials, but the joy lies beyond these.

Again, Jesus modeled what to do. Despite deteriorating relationships with His enemies, He persevered in sharing the same good news He had shared from the beginning: "The time has come," he said. "The kingdom of God has come near. Turn away from your sins and believe the good news!" (Mark 1:15 NIRV)

> ### Lesson learned #45:
> Persevere in sharing the good news, no matter how our enemies resist.

And His enemies' attitude led to increasing hostility and belligerent reaction against His message.

> Once again the people picked up stones to kill him. Jesus said, "At my Father's direction I have done many good works. For which one are you going to stone me?" They replied, "We're stoning you not for any good work, but for blasphemy! You, a mere man, claim to be God" John 10:31-33 (NLT).

Instead of hating them, as we might, Jesus proposed a radical solution in Matthew 5:43-45 (NASB): "You have heard that it was said, 'You shall love your neighbor and hate your enemy.' But I say to you, love your enemies and pray for those who persecute you, so that you may be sons of your Father who is in heaven."

Lesson learned #46:

Loving enemies is never easy, but Jesus commands it. And when we do, He builds not only our love, but also our patience. *That's* perseverance.

So, how did Jesus demonstrate this true love through forgiveness? As He hung on the cross, Jesus showed Himself to be the Savior, praying, "Father, forgive them, for they do not know what they are doing" (Luke 23:34 NIV).

In an act of love on the cross, Jesus forgave His enemies! What a beautiful example of love in action! That Jesus' **first** recorded saying from the cross concerned forgiveness is humbling indeed.

Lesson learned #47:

In His love, Jesus forgave even those who didn't want a relationship with Him!

We can also learn much from Jesus' relationships with His disciples.

Jesus forgave His disciples

Jesus forgiving Peter is among the Bible's most poignant moments. Just before His agonizing time in Gethsemane, Jesus predicted that Peter would deny Him.

> Then Jesus told them, "This very night you will all fall away on account of me, for it is written:
>> 'I will strike the shepherd,
>> and the sheep of the flock will be scattered.'
>
> But after I have risen, I will go ahead of you into Galilee."
> Peter replied, "Even if all fall away on account of you, I never will."
> "Truly I tell you," Jesus answered, "this very night, before the rooster crows, you will disown me three times."
> Matthew 26:31-34 (NIV)

Sadly, just as He foretold, Peter denied Jesus three times.

> But Peter said, "Man, I don't know what you're talking about!" Just then, while he was still speaking, a rooster crowed. Then the Lord turned and looked straight at Peter. And Peter remembered the word from the Lord, and how he had told him, "Before a rooster crows today, you will deny me three times." So he went outside and cried bitterly.
> Luke 22:60-62 (ISV)

And in one of Scripture's tenderest moments, Jesus forgives Peter, restoring him and giving him a major assignment.

> When they had finished eating, Jesus said to Simon Peter, "Simon son of John, do you love me more than these?"
> "Yes, Lord," he said, "you know that I love you."
> Jesus said, "Feed my lambs."
> Again Jesus said, "Simon son of John, do you love me?"
> He answered, "Yes, Lord, you know that I love you."
> Jesus said, "Take care of my sheep."
> The third time he said to him, "Simon son of John, do you love me?"
> Peter was hurt because Jesus asked him the third time, "Do you love me?" He said, "Lord, you know all things; you know that I love you."
> Jesus said, "Feed my sheep." John 21:15-17 (NIV)

Peter received not only the joy of being forgiven but also the joy of being commissioned to witness to thousands of others (Acts 2:41).

Lesson learned #48:
When we forgive others, especially those closest to us, we please God and impact His kingdom in unimaginable ways!

Jesus' relationship with His Father

God knew that humankind could never save itself: we could never offer a sufficient payment for our sinful nature. And because He is equally loving and just, God cannot just "look past" sin — Someone had to pay. So in His wisdom, God conceived a plan to save humans from their sin by making Christ a suitable sacrifice. "For God made Christ, who never sinned, to be the offering for our sin, so that we could be made right with God through Christ" (2 Corinthians 5:21 NLT).

And Christ's relationship with the Father was so perfect and His love for us so deep that, in obedience to the Father, He came to earth to spill His blood for the forgiveness of sin. "And he took a cup, and when he had given thanks he gave it to them, saying, 'Drink of it, all of you, for this is my blood of the covenant, which is poured out for many for the forgiveness of sins'" (Matthew 26:27-28 ESV).

That forgiveness is His unfathomable love for us, which the apostle John defines: "This is love: not that we loved God, but that he loved us and sent his Son as an atoning sacrifice for our sins" (1 John 4:10 NIV).

The evidence is overwhelming: Jesus knew joy, because He forgave in His relationships.

Here's how forgiveness helped me know joy in one of my closest relationships.

My Journey to Joy

Family Relationships

My motto is straightforward. There's nothing more important to me than my relationships: Jesus, Suzanne, our kids, our family, and our friends. So building solid relationships is a top priority. Most of the time, my relationships go well.

But sometimes they crash and burn.

My most challenging family relationship was with my Dad's father, Bob Zimmerman. Granddad didn't have time for his family. He worked the nightshift at the factory so that he could avoid his wife and my Dad. And he was smooth as silk with people outside of his family, but bitter towards those who loved him most. For years I managed a fragile relationship by flattering him. As I got older, I realized that our relationship was one-way, so I went cold-turkey on the false compliments. Guess what happened to the relationship?

For several years, our relationship floundered. But when Granddad's kidneys failed, necessitating dialysis, and he could no longer live alone, God gave me a tenderness towards this now shrunken husk of a man.

In short, through God's grace, I forgave Granddad.

No, Granddad didn't treat me or my family better. In fact, as he got sicker and frailer, he treated us even worse.

Yet the more he mistreated me, the easier it became to forgive him. I prayed more fervently that God would provide an opportunity for me to talk to Granddad about Christ. Yes, at times his behavior angered me, but God's loving forgiveness prevailed and paid big dividends.

After several years in and out of the hospital, Granddad was finally approaching death. Each time I had a chance to witness to him, I got cold feet. I can witness to complete strangers, but when it comes to family members, I'm often paralyzed.

Lesson learned #49:
If you find it's hardest to evangelize to family members, don't let that stop you! Ask God for the courage and the timing to accomplish what He wants.

Finally, God arranged a perfect opportunity. Granddad had been in and out of consciousness for a week, but when I visited him this particular afternoon, he was as clear-headed as he used to be.

The Holy Spirit prompted me: "Now!"

My hands shook as I held his cold hands. My eyes met his and I saw he was lucid and could understand.

Me:	Granddad, I want to ask you something.
Granddad:	What?
Me:	Do you know who Jesus Christ is?
Granddad:	Yes, I do.
Me:	*(hands shaking even more)* Do you know that to be saved you simply need to confess your sins and accept His free gift of life?
Granddad:	Yes, I do.
Me:	Would you like to accept Jesus into your heart now?
Granddad:	Yes, I would.

With that, I led him in a short prayer that he repeated. After he accepted Christ, I closed by reciting Psalm 23, and Granddad joined in right away.

Tears of joy!

And all this sprang from forgiveness. If I hadn't forgiven him, I would not have known the joy of seeing him saved. To this day, I have such joy in knowing Granddad is with Jesus!

Granddad passed two days later at age 89 — a deathbed conversion for sure. He had already asked me to lead his celebration of life service and, for the first time in my life with him, it was a joy to serve him!

Lesson learned #50:
Don't let your pride get in the way of your relationships.

God worked through forgiveness to bring the greatest joy ever to my Granddad: eternal salvation in Jesus!

Broken relationships

Grandad was my most broken *family* relationship, but I have had an even more broken relationship than that.

Sure, there was that time I got a little too opinionated at a Bible study and essentially broke up the group. Everyone gracefully accepted my apology, but I still wince at my example of how *not* to handle conflict. And there have been a few bosses who made our jobs miserable for us by playing favorites, advancing questionable agendas, and acting in curious ways.

But when I survey the landscape of all my relationships past and present, I reach an embarrassing conclusion…

My most broken relationship was with Jesus.

We started strong when I surrendered my life to Him at age 8. But there was a LONG span of years (16 to be exact) when I wandered far from Him. (My poor excuses for wandering, and how God gracefully brought me back, are the topic of another guide I'm writing.) In order for our relationship to be restored I had to first confess my habitual sin. And Jesus completely forgave me. He is so good like that: He forgives us of our sin. He responds to us just as He did to the woman caught in adultery in John 8:10-11.

> Jesus straightened up and asked her, "Woman, where are they? Has no one condemned you?"
> "No one, sir," she said.
> "Then neither do I condemn you," Jesus declared. "Go now and leave your life of sin."

Jesus wasn't assuming we'll never sin again. He *was* saying that we must leave our sinful choices behind and follow Him. But during those 16 years, I often thought, "I just don't feel close to God right now."

Then, during a men's retreat one time, Pastor Dan Erickson engaged us with this provocative thought: "As a pastor, I often hear people say, 'You know, I just don't feel close to God right now.' And I'll usually respond like this, 'You say you don't feel close to God, but I have one question for you…WHO MOVED?!'"

Convicted!

Because of my sinful choices, I caused my most broken relationship: with Jesus. But because of His restoring power, I once again had the joy of a close relationship with Him.

> ### <u>Lesson learned #51:</u>
> We move away from God; He never abandons us. Joy awaits you as you move closer in right relationship with Him.

And that's why I can sadly say that my most broken relationship was with Jesus.

Maybe you're like me? Do you sense that *your* most broken relationship is with Jesus?

<u>Your Journey to Joy</u>

JOY CHALLENGE #5: Consider how you can know joy through your most broken relationship.

CHAPTER 5 QUESTIONS:
1. Why are relationships so important to God? To us?
2. How has forgiveness impacted your relationships?
3. Jesus forgave His enemies, so how can we forgive our enemies?
4. Who in your life do you need to forgive?
5. Do you sense that your most broken relationship is with Jesus? If not, what's your most broken relationship?
6. Explain in 30 seconds, how did it get so broken? What can you do to help repair it?
7. Which lesson was most helpful to you? Why?

Psalms of Joy

The LORD *is my shepherd; I shall not want.*

He maketh me to lie down in green pastures: he leadeth me beside the still waters.

He restoreth my soul: he leadeth me in the paths of righteousness for his name's sake.

Yea, though I walk through the valley of the shadow of death, I will fear no evil: for thou art with me; thy rod and thy staff they comfort me.

Thou preparest a table before me in the presence of mine enemies: thou anointest my head with oil; my cup runneth over.

Surely goodness and mercy shall follow me all the days of my life: and I will dwell in the house of the LORD *forever.*

Psalm 23:1-6 KJV

Jesus' Journey to Joy®

Chapter 6

Jesus knew joy because He promised in the death of a loved one.
(Luke 23:38-43)

6

JOY IN THE DEATH OF A LOVED ONE

Jesus answered him, "Truly I tell you, today you will be with me in paradise."
Luke 23:43 (NIV) (Jesus' second statement from the cross)

You're born. You suffer. You die. Fortunately, there's a loophole.
~ Billy Graham

Jesus knew joy because He promised in the death of a loved one.

His promise: don't delay, choose today!

Before noon on the first Good Friday, Jesus and two criminals were on full display before the onlookers assembled to witness His crucifixion. Here, in His **second** of seven recorded sayings on the cross, Jesus promised a repentant thief, whom He loved (John 3:16), the glory that awaited him.

> There was a written notice above him, which read: THIS IS THE KING OF THE JEWS.
> One of the criminals who hung there hurled insults at him: "Aren't you the Messiah? Save yourself and us!"
> But the other criminal rebuked him. "Don't you fear God," he said, "since you are under the same sentence? We are punished justly, for we are getting what our deeds deserve. But this man has done nothing wrong."
> Then he said, "Jesus, remember me when you come into your kingdom."

Jesus answered him, "Truly I tell you, today you will be with me in paradise." Luke 23:38-43 (NIV)

Magnificent! This account of two criminals headed in spiritually opposite directions reflects the decision each one of us must make: choosing or losing Christ. The first criminal rejects Jesus, but the second criminal received Jesus' promise of eternal life. Talk about a last-minute decision of eternal significance!

In my pastoral experience, I occasionally encounter people who have the "best of both worlds" approach.

• I'm going to live my life for myself, and then, at the end of it...

• I'm going to choose Christ now, like the second criminal did.

The "best of both worlds"? No such thing! This naive approach could ultimately mean eternal death, because...

1. It assumes that you *know* the day of your death. Who wakes up knowing that?
2. It assumes that living for yourself, rather than for Christ, is the better option.

Lesson learned #52:

The same eternal life Jesus promised to the second thief is available to you today (see John 3:16). Why risk your eternal life on the flawed "best of both worlds" approach when you can choose eternal joy in Jesus now?

And here at His cross, Jesus imparts another lesson of highest joy.

Lesson learned #53:

The death of a loved one (the second criminal) points to the death of *the* One — Jesus — who died for all. His death was vilest torture and agony, but the true joy that it brought is sublime! (More on this in Chapter 11 Joy in Dying to Self.)

JOY IN THE DEATH OF A LOVED ONE

Comforting those who've experienced the death of a loved one.

When a loved one dies, it is vital to care for others who've also experienced that loss. In a tender passage (John 11:17-37), Jesus comforted Mary and Martha even as He shared in their grief. He spent time with them, empathized with them, reassured them, and even wept with them!

Jesus never failed to comfort hurting people, but I fall far short of the mark here. Sometimes I am so wrapped up in myself that I neglect to empathize with people I love most. Let me give you an example.

My entire family, and especially my Mom, Susette, agreed that Dad's frontotemporal death was the most brutal death we'd ever seen. Words can't describe the suffering we endured, most of all Dad. It was like a tornado raging into our house — our lives — for three years, leaving death, destruction, and depression in its wake.

And then the tornado was gone.

And so was Dad.

But the feelings of loss remained like an uninvited guest who's overstayed his welcome.

In the immediate wake of Dad's death, I felt grief. But mostly I felt relief that he no longer suffered and joy that he was now with Jesus, fully healed. So, I shared my joy with Mom the night of his passing:

Me: Mom, we're all going to miss Dad, but I am so thankful that God took him home. Dad no longer suffers, no longer stumbles. He's in the presence of our Lord Jesus, fully restored. We have so much joy!

Mom: (*silence*)

As I would learn in the months after Dad's passing, I jumped straight to joy because I wanted everyone – including Mom – to be encouraged that Dad was now healed. But I made a terrible mistake: I wasn't meeting Mom where she was in her grief. And, I realize in retrospect, I was ignoring my own grief.

> ### **Lesson learned #54:**
> In comforting someone who's lost a loved one, avoid being either too joyous or too morose. Allow God to guide you in that tricky middle ground. That brings comfort and joy that's both real and helpful.

Shortest Scripture, biggest love

Jesus experienced joy in the death of a loved one when He raised Lazarus from the grave. But He had to first pass through deepest sorrow over His friend's death. John recounts in 11:33-35 (NASB):

"When Jesus therefore saw her weeping, and the Jews who came with her *also* weeping, He was deeply moved in spirit and was troubled, and said, 'Where have you laid him?' They said to Him, 'Lord, come and see.' Jesus wept."

The Bible's shortest verse (John 11:35) speaks not just of His sorrow, but of the biggest love behind that sorrow. This leads us to another lesson.

> ### **Lesson learned #55:**
> Jesus models for us that we, too, often must pass through deepest sorrow to get to joy.

We know that Jesus experienced the death of a loved one; and even bystander Jews recognized His love for Lazarus in John 11:36 (CSB): "So the Jews said, 'See how he loved him!'"

This is a critical truth we don't want to miss. Just as Jesus deeply loved Lazarus, Jesus loves you with the same passionate love! He created you, after all! Meditate on this truth until you experience it with the "eyes of your understanding." It's one thing to see a 5x7 picture of the Grand

Canyon. But it's an entirely different experience to actually stand there in front of it, taking in God's breathtaking beauty!

Lesson learned #56:

Jesus loves you beyond measure; you are precious to Him beyond compare!

Knowing that truth leads us to another priceless truth: He doesn't want *any* one of us to die without Him.

- "For I take no delight in the death of anyone, declares the Sovereign LORD. Repent and live!" Ezekiel 18:32 (NET)

- Instead he is patient with you, not wanting anyone to perish, but everyone to come to repentance. 2 Peter 3:9 (NIV)

Lesson learned #57:

God doesn't desire the death of *any* loved one (that's us!), so repent and live in joy!

Indeed, on our Journey to Joy, we, like Jesus, can experience joy even in the death of a loved one.

My Journey to Joy

Years ago, my son Grant's 4th birthday balloon escaped his grasp and floated up into the blue sky. Then, heart wrenching crying for 20 minutes. Our oldest son Koen, eight at the time, mused, "I think the saddest thing in the world is seeing a balloon float away and hearing a kid crying about it." The wisdom of a child!

The death of a loved one can be like that, too, except we adults hide our emotions better. Or not.

"The C Word"

It's one of those life-changing events you never forget.

- The thrill of soloing on my bike, no training wheels (March 1975)
- The pain of having my impacted wisdom teeth pulled (April 1986)
- The day Mom called to tell me she had cancer (June 2005)

I hung up the phone, stunned by the awful news: Mom had "The C Word." The bathroom offered our house's only privacy. I quickly locked the door and bawled my eyes out.

Mom's fight ultimately lasted several years. During that time three of her dearest loved ones also suffered tragedies.

1. Dad was diagnosed with frontotemporal dementia and needed Mom's help.
2. Granddad (Dad's father) had kidney failure but refused assisted living care and needed Mom's help.
3. I lost my second job and needed Mom's financial help.

In less than a month, Dad's forced retirement brought him home to stay. Not only that, Granddad couldn't take care of himself, so Dad, in his mental illness, invited his father to stay at their house. Mom was working full-time, so an ill father-in-law was a tremendous burden on her: two sick, demanding men consumed with their own troubles and relying on Mom to put her troubles on hold to care for them. To get a sense of the craziness, in the same day:

- Dad soiled his pants.

- Granddad lost control of his dialysis machine and bled all over the living room sofa and carpet.

- Mom vomited from her treatments.

Mom once deadpanned that she, Dad, and Granddad were in a race to see who would die first.

At one point, my brother Eric dropped by Mom's house only to find her collapsed on the ground from exhaustion. She had worn herself out caring for others! Mom may not have known it, but she lived out Jesus' words of Mark 10:43-44 (NIV), "But it is not this way among you, but whoever wishes to become great among you shall be your servant; and whoever wishes to be first among you shall be slave of all."

Mom certainly wasn't seeking greatness, yet her actions taught us all a valuable lesson.

Lesson learned #58:

Even in dying, Mom served others first. She continually put herself before her dying husband, her dying father-in-law, her nearly bankrupt son, and others. It was her joy to do so; she would not have it any other way! For those of us who aren't imminently dying it ought to be a little easier to be a slave of all.

Courageously fighting battles

If there could have been a silver lining, it was that thyroid cancer is considered by many experts to be among the most curable. However, we learned years later that Mom's cancer had metastasized about ten years before detection: it had a head start medicine couldn't overcome.

By God's grace, Mom took her cancer fight in stride, diligently pursuing treatment options wherever her specialists sent her. And for the first few years, all of us, especially Mom, held out hope that she truly was going to beat back this monster invading her body. She projected such a marvelous attitude, often quipping about the need to "keep on keeping on!" It was a joy to fight the good fight with her!

Yet dark times continued. She committed Dad to a memory care unit in 2010, one day before her own open-heart surgery to fight the cancer that had spread to her pericardium. Dad passed in 2011 (you can read that account and the lessons learned in *A Faithful Dad's Guide to Legacy*); Granddad passed in 2013.

After twelve surgeries, radiation, dietary changes, and other traditional methods failed to stem cancer's onslaught, Mom sought help from experimental treatments at Penn State Hershey Medical Center, Johns Hopkins, and the University of Maryland. All along the way, Mom inspired her family, friends, coworkers, and medical professionals. A note from a dear friend spoke for us all:

> Oh, I want to hug you, Susette..... xoxoxoxo My prayers are there for comfort and peace as you look to Jesus.... You have been such a wonderful friend through the years, such an example of love, courage, ambition, and everything that's good. I love you. J. H.

Asked how she felt after a particular treatment, Mom joked, "I feel like I got kicked in the mouth by a horse, but other than that, I feel great!" After nine years of fighting, Mom's options ran out — long before her determination did. Outside her hospital room, the oncologist, a palliative care doc, a resident, and a nurse discussed her situation. They quietly filed into Mom's room, gathering around her bed to inform her that there was a large amount of fluid in her lungs. In fact, she had witnessed the actual swallowing test for herself earlier that morning. The team explained what they could do to drain it.

Mom took a deep breath and sighed.

Firmly, but with a smile on her face, she announced, "Listen, I'm not stupid. I know that I'm out of options. And I'm not afraid. I saw with my own eyes *exactly* why I'm choking every time I try to eat or drink. I saw the liquid I swallowed go right down my windpipe. I'm aspirating on ICE CHIPS!!! Every time I elected for surgery, radiation, or a new drug, I did it because there was hope for curing me. I am out of options. I don't want to be bitter or act out against those I love."
The palliative care doctor exclaimed, "Mrs. Zimmerman, you have a smile on your face!"

Mom replied, "You know, you wake up every day. Some days you are happy; some days you are sad or grumpy. It's up to you how you choose to live that day. You can grouch around or you can put on a smile. I choose to put on a smile [long pause].... "I think I was born happy."

> ### Lesson learned #59:
> Mom's response and her life spoke volumes about her character! Rather than become bitter or act out against those she loved, she chose happiness! Whether we're fighting for our life or not, we can choose joy, too!

After the room cleared, we huddled together to learn Mom's final wishes.

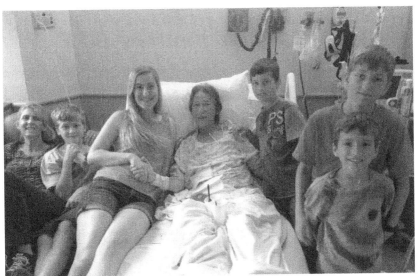

Relishing her family relationships, Mom fought bravely.

A Deathbed Defeat

As I wrote in her obit, "Susette L. Zimmerman, 63, of Fayetteville, PA, passed into Christ's glory on Thursday, July 24, 2014 (at 12:10 a.m.)." My wife, Suzanne, and I arrived soon after her death.

The elevator opened, and I pushed Suzanne's wheelchair into Mom's room, almost afraid of what we would find. There, in the middle of her private room, lay Mom lifeless. I felt hopeless. Surreal.

I watched her still face. Her death had been nine years in coming, but how could she be gone so soon?

My phone rang: it was an organ donation representative confirming Mom's decision to donate her corneas for research. What a generous way to help others. I noticed now just how frail she looked.

Suzanne and I sat in the silence of Mom's room for a long time, quietly crying, barely speaking. Just after 2:30 a.m., my phone rang: organ donation again. "Mr. Zimmerman," the representative explained, "I'm so sorry, but because of the extent of your mother's cancer, we are unable to accept her corneas."

The cancer had ravaged Mom's body for nine years, and it showed. And *that's* when the Spirit whispered a sobering lesson.

Lesson learned #60:
"The cancer in Mom's body was winning…until it lost."

Mom's body was completely spent; not even research could salvage *any* value. The cancer devoured her — until it met with its own deathbed defeat. Jesus had fully restored Mom in His presence and cancer died: absolute joy amidst deepest sorrow. The Spirit immediately revealed another lesson.

Lesson learned #61:
"At Calvary, Satan thought he was winning…until he lost!"

Truth! The devil stood no chance against Christ, who victoriously rose from the dead! Recall the words of 1 Corinthians 15:55,57 (NIV): "Where, O death, is your victory? Where, O death, is your sting? But thanks be to God! He gives us the victory through our Lord Jesus Christ."

Mom may be gone, but the lessons both God and she taught me in her passing — and in her eternal life — deepen my desire to meet them both face-to-face! I can only imagine!

For several years I grieved terribly over the loss of both parents at age 63. I had a series of nightmares, too. But at last the Holy Spirit brought peace to my aching heart. He shared these soothing words with me:

> **"I know you are heartbroken over the loss of your parents. But if you could catch a glimpse of them, as if looking through a peephole into heaven, you would be so delighted by what you would see! Your dad and mom are with Me, and they are *more* than perfect, because they are both in My presence. I have fully restored them. Have peace in Me."**

His words quelled my tears. I whispered into the darkness, "In other words, God, I'm not crying for them, because they're perfect, *better* than perfect! I'm crying for myself, because I miss them."

Yes!

When we experience the death of a loved one, crying, self-reflection, and sometimes nightmares are part of the grieving process. You can't put grieving on a time table; it won't be rushed. But in that time table, God can teach us a lesson in joy that we'll never forget.

Lesson learned #62:

The Lord reassures us through His Word that our departed loved ones who loved Christ are beyond good, and that we will be, too.

Your Journey to Joy

JOY CHALLENGE #6: Reflect on how you can know joy in the death of a loved one.

CHAPTER 6 QUESTIONS:

1. Why is the "best of both worlds" approach (live for myself now, choose Christ just before I die) naive?
2. In light of Jesus' promise of eternal life, how does that affect the way you live your life now?
3. Jesus models for us that we, too, often must pass through deepest sorrow to get to joy. What examples can you share from your own life?
4. "At Calvary, Satan thought he was winning...until he lost!" How so?
5. Which lesson was most helpful to you? Why?
6. How can you comfort someone who has suffered the death of a loved one?

PART 3

JOY THROUGH INNER TRIALS

*"Through Joseph, we learn how suffering, no matter how unfair,
develops strong character and deep wisdom."*
~ NIV Life Application Study Bible *Genesis 37, preamble*

Jesus' Journey to Joy®

Chapter 7

Jesus knew joy because He planned for rejection.
(Luke 19:26-27)

7

JOY IN REJECTION

When Jesus then saw His mother, and the disciple whom He loved standing nearby, He said to His mother, "Woman, behold, your son!" Then He said to the disciple, "Behold, your mother!" From that hour the disciple took her into his own household. John 19:26-27 (NASB) (Jesus' third statement from the cross)

I tell ya, when I was a kid, all I knew was rejection. My yo-yo, it never came back! ~ Rodney Dangerfield

> ## Jesus knew joy because He planned for rejection.

The cross stood as the brutal physical reality of the world rejecting Jesus. Yet despite the agony and pain the cross offered, Jesus, in His **third** recorded saying from the cross, planned not only for His rejection but also for His mother. As we saw above in the verses from John 19, the apostle recounts how Jesus, even while He was hanging on the cross, instructed John to take care of His mother.

Jesus frequently encountered rejection, so He was certainly no stranger to it. From the earliest times — literally — humans have rejected God. We could say that Jesus planned for rejection, because we humans reject God all too frequently. Here are a few sad, but eventually joyful, examples of how humans have rejected God.

The First Rejection

Location: The Garden of Eden (Genesis 2:8)

The blessing: God blessed [Adam and Eve] and said, "Have many children and grow in number. Fill the earth and be its master. Rule over the fish in the sea and over the birds in the sky and over every living thing that moves on the earth" Genesis 1:28 (NCV).

Situation: God placed Adam in the Garden with only one command: "You must not eat from the tree of the knowledge of good and evil, for on the day you eat from it, you will certainly die" Genesis 2:17 (CSB).

Question: At our daily breakfast devotional, one of my kids once asked me, "Daddy, how long do you think it was from when God told Adam and Eve not to eat the apple until they actually ate it?" Think on that one for a while!

Regardless of how long it took, Eve, and then Adam, enticed by the serpent Satan, rejected God's sole command: "The woman was convinced. How lovely and fresh looking it was! And it would make her so wise! So she ate some of the fruit and gave some to her husband, and he ate it too" Genesis 3:6 (TLB).

The curse: God cursed the serpent (Genesis 3:14), Eve (Genesis 3:16), and Adam (Genesis 3:17).

Lesson learned #63:
The joy in the first rejection is that God initiated His rescue plan, often named the protoevangelium (first gospel) in Genesis 3:15. That rejection foreshadowed the rejection of Christ ("My Father, why have You forsaken me?"). God cursed the first Adam, foreshadowing how He cursed the Second Adam for our sake.

Therefore, in the Garden of Eden, we see that God turned humans' rejection of Him into a plan for His joy: Jesus Christ coming to earth to save humankind. However, before Christ would come, Israel would repeatedly reject their God for hundreds of years.

A Series of Rejections

Throughout the Old Testament humans rejected God.

- **Desert Rejection**: "Now the LORD will give you meat, and you will eat it. You will not eat it for just one day, or two days, or five, ten or twenty days, but for a whole month — until it comes out of your nostrils and you loathe it — **because you have rejected the LORD,** who is among you, and have wailed before him, saying, 'Why did we ever leave Egypt?'" Numbers 11:18-20 (NIV)

- **The Royal Rejection**: "But when [the Israelites] said, 'Give us a king to lead us,' this displeased Samuel; so he prayed to the LORD. And the LORD told him: 'Listen to all that the people are saying to you; **it is not you they have rejected, but they have rejected me as their king**.'" 1 Samuel 8:6-7 (NIV)

- **Mankind's Rejection**: Seven hundred years before it happened, Isaiah prophesied that humanity would reject Christ: "He was despised and rejected…" Isaiah 53:3 (NLT). Yet within this same rejection prophecy, Isaiah proclaimed the joy that will arise from Jesus' rejection: "When he [Jesus] sees all that is accomplished by his anguish, he will be satisfied. And because of his experience, my righteous servant will make it possible for many to be counted righteous, for he will bear all their sins." Isaiah 53:11 (NLT)

Lesson learned #64:

Throughout history, humans have rejected God, so our approach to Him is cause for humility and planning. God always loves us, but for us to *love* God we first must *accept* God as who He claims to be. We love Him because He first loved us (1 John 4:19 WEB).

The apostle John foreshadows Christ's rejection in John 1:9-11 (ESV): "The true light, which gives light to everyone, was coming into the world. He was in the world, and the world was made through him, yet the world did not know him. He came to his own, and his own people did not receive him."

We've reviewed what others have said about His rejection, but what did Jesus Himself say about it?

What Jesus said about HIS rejection

Let's be candid: Jesus had many enemies; He still does. The apostle John told us, "He came to his own people, and even they rejected him" (1:11 NLT). In short, His own rejected Him, but how Jesus handled His relationships with His enemies is instructive to us.

Immediately after Jesus announced His public ministry, He received initial acceptance. However, that soon turned to anger and rejection. Luke records this reality in 4:28-29 (NIV): "All the people in the synagogue were furious when they heard this. They got up, drove him out of the town, and took him to the brow of the hill on which the town was built, in order to throw him off the cliff."

Again, we see the good news that Jesus came into the world and His public ministry was fully proclaimed, but His own rejected Him. Jesus speaks in several passages about His rejection.

- "Haven't you read this Scripture: The stone that the builders **rejected** has become the cornerstone." Mark 12:10 (CSB)

- "The Son of Man must suffer a great deal and be **rejected** by the elders, the high priests, and the scribes. Then he must be killed, but on the third day he will be raised." Luke 9:22 (ISV)

- "But first He must suffer many things and be **rejected** by this generation." Luke 17:25 (HCSB)

Just as Jesus taught, many continued to reject Him throughout His ministry, even up to His time on the cross.

- Then the entire town came out to meet Jesus. When they saw him, they begged him to leave their region. Matthew 8:34 (EHV)

- Then they scoffed, "He's just a carpenter, the son of Mary and the brother of James, Joseph, Judas, and Simon. And his sisters live right here among us." They were deeply offended and refused to believe in him. Mark 6:3 (NLT)

We could too easily conclude that Jesus' earthly ministry ended as it began, in rejection. At first we might think there was a hopeful reversal of His rejection at Nazareth, because the Palm Sunday crowds initially accepted Jesus as He rode into Jerusalem on a donkey. John records in 12:12-13 (NRSV), "The next day a great crowd who had come to the feast heard that Jesus was coming to Jerusalem. So they took branches of palm trees and went out to meet him, crying, 'Hosanna! Blessed is he who comes in the name of the Lord, even the King of Israel!'"

However, His Palm Sunday acceptance lasted barely a week, and by the Preparation of Passover another crowd was in a rage. So instead of a reversal, we see a sobering parallel to His early rejection: at the end of His earthly ministry, Luke recounts, a crowd was shouting, "Kill Jesus! Give us Barabbas!" (John 23:18 CEV)

In fact, many continued to reject Him even while He hung on the cross! Matthew sadly records in 27:41-42 (AMP), "In the same way the chief priests also, along with the scribes and elders, mocked Him, saying, 'He saved others [from death]; He cannot save Himself. He is the King of Israel; let Him now come down from the cross, and we will believe in Him *and* acknowledge Him.'"

Prophecy foretold of Jesus' rejection, and Jesus Himself spoke of His rejection. Did Jesus also prepare His disciples for rejection? Absolutely!

What Jesus said about OUR rejection

Here are some key teachings on the rejection Jesus promises His followers will experience because of Him.

Guilt by association (with Jesus): You WILL be rejected

Jesus' upper room teaching puts it plainly:

> If the world hates you, realize that it hated me before it hated you. If you had anything in common with the world, the world

would love you as one of its own. But you don't have anything in common with the world. I chose you from the world, and that's why the world hates you. (John 15:18-19 GW)

After Jesus ascended, several of His disciples experienced rejection at the hands of the Sanhedrin. Luke chronicles,

> They called the apostles in and had them flogged. Then they ordered them not to speak in the name of Jesus, and let them go. The apostles left the Sanhedrin, **rejoicing** because they had been counted worthy of suffering disgrace for the Name. (Acts 5:40-41 NIV).

Lesson learned #65:

Just as the apostles modeled Jesus' joy in rejection, so we can take joy in the "floggings" we endure in the marketplace, in our personal lives, or anywhere else we face persecution.

Stand firm until the end

In a popularity-driven culture it's hard to go against the crowd. But that is *exactly* what Jesus is asking us to do in Matthew 10:22 (TLV): "You will be hated by everyone because of my name. But the one who holds out to the end will be delivered." And that deliverance brings us joy.

It's hard to be hated. But when Jesus promises we will be saved if we stand firm with Him until the end, He is really talking about us joyfully persevering. That ties in directly with our guide's key Scripture, James 1:2 (NIV), "**Consider it pure joy, my brothers and sisters, whenever you face trials of many kinds.**"

We strengthen our foundation by facing trials of many kinds, including rejection. And *that* supports our main premise: **Joy is knowing Jesus, walking with Him through all our trials.** We come face-to-face with this reality: joy and trials are intertwined. To persevere with Jesus we stand firm until the end! And that end will include a judgement.

Judgement day is coming

Don't judge me!" This is a common retort aimed at anyone who doesn't tolerate a particular decision, lifestyle, or action. And yet, by virtue of who God is, Jesus speaks of the inevitable judgment to come in John 12:48 (LEB): "The one who rejects me and does not accept my words has one who judges him; the word that I have spoken will judge him on the last day."

Could Jesus have been any clearer in what He's asking us to do?

> ### Lesson learned #66:
> You WILL be rejected. The question is, will you choose God's rejection or the world's rejection?

No, rejection is never easy, and this next story of rejection will make you wince.

My Journey to Joy

Rejection stories can be so awful that something which happened thirty years ago *still* sticks in your memory. This is one of those stories.

Dog Show Dreams

The requirement seemed so simple, a piece of cake. To earn the Boy Scouts of America Pets Merit Badge, all you really had to do was show your pet in a pet show. What better way for a ninth grader like me to shine, just me and my dog, Vinnie?

I found an upcoming dog show competition a few miles from my house. We only had a couple weeks to practice, though, so Vinnie and I needed to get working on our pet show routine.

Vinnie was a purebred Gordon Setter, a hunting dog through and through. With "dogged" perseverance and a supply of large Milk-Bones, my brother and I trained Vinnie to do a few standard tricks pretty well:

sit, stay, shake, and (my favorite), speak! Exactly the tricks dog show judges want to see, right?

The mid-July Saturday of the dog show dawned hotter than a Texas skillet. I sprang from my bunk bed and grabbed my Mad Magazine Alfred E. Neuman "What, me worry?" T-shirt. Dog show casual for sure.

As I raced to fetch Vinnie from his dog pen, I reviewed my well-planned dog show routine.

1. I would tell Vinnie to sit. People like that.
2. I would tell him to shake. People love that. I was getting pumped!
3. I would tell Vinnie to stay. People would be in suspense by the time I set up my grand trick.
4. The finale: I'd walk a few paces ahead of Vinnie, turn around and command, "Vinnie, SPEAK!"

And Vinnie would *speak*. A bark for the ages, a bark that would be my dog's championship roar!

Dog Show Day

We ran through our routine again. When it was time to head to the show, I loaded Vinnie into the back of our Oldsmobile, Mom buckled up at the wheel, and off we went. Fifteen minutes later we arrived at the school hosting the dog show. All those cars, trucks, and dogs! I'd never been to a dog show....

Mom and I leashed Vinnie and hurried to the registration table. Vinnie lagged behind us, spooked by all the other show dogs. I practically had to drag him along. That should have been a red flag.

After a little hunting, we found our category. Wow, only ONE other Gordon Setter had been entered into the show. There was definitely a chance for glory, maybe first place, or even best of show!

Dragging Vinnie behind, Mom and I went to watch the dogs in other categories until ours was called.

That's when the beads of sweat began to pore off my head — and not because it was a sweltering day.

Some dogs were navigating obstacle courses, some were walking close to their owners, and some looked like they'd been trained by cyborgs, obedient to the death. I didn't see a single dog perform any of Vinnie's moves: sit, shake, stay, and speak. Actually, the only sounds we heard were owners barking out commands to their dogs. It seemed no dogs barked anywhere on the show grounds.

"Well," I reasoned, "at least it'll be quiet when they hear Vinnie bark in his final championship routine!"

Mom interrupted my daydreams: the Gordon Setter category was up next. Since we signed up second, we'd go second. And I liked going last because you can gauge your competition and plan how to win.

Joan and Bridget

The other Gordon Setter owner was an American Kennel Club breeder I'll call "Joan." Our family had visited Joan's Pennsylvania kennels; but we fell in love with Vinnie, who came from a Virginia kennel.

At the announcer's call, Joan entered the judging area with her Setter, Bridget. Joan performed a brisk run-walk with Bridget smoothly in step at every 90-degree turn. After her first lap, Joan stood stock still. Bridget sat at her side, looked up and waited for her next command.

I was really sweating by now. "Yeah, but can Bridget speak?" I tried to calm myself.

"Bridget, heel!" Joan rasped sharply. Bridget stuck to her like glue, attention fixed on Joan.

Not a single one of her tricks was one Vinnie and I had practiced. When they finished, people clapped loudly and nodded approvingly.

I was getting a sinking feeling.

Duo Disaster

"Travis Zimmerman and his Gordon Setter, Vinnie," the announcer proclaimed.

I swallowed hard and stepped onto the grounds. I felt all eyes on Vinnie and me.

In a split second I changed to an impromptu routine. Copying Joan and Bridget, I started an unplanned gallop. Somehow I thought Vinnie would follow me. I gave him Milk-Bones, didn't I?

As I looked straight ahead and ran, the slack in Vinnie's leash suddenly drew taught. I fell and my head swiveled unnaturally backwards. There was Vinnie, refusing to budge. Gasps from the crowd. I felt my face grow red. Vinnie was as agitated as I was, but I decided to try another Joan trick. Even if I had to skip most of what we'd practiced, I was determined to finish with Vinnie's championship bark.

In my cracking, pubescent voice, I looked down at my poor dog and commanded, "Vinnie, heel!"

He wouldn't budge. More disapproving groans from the crowd. And some snickers?

I glowered at Vinnie, even as his pitiful eyes begged me to stop this disaster.

Eyebrows furrowed, I raised my voice to fever pitch, "Vinnie, HEEL!"

Vinnie sat there, his sad eyes taking in his master gone mad.

Desperately I yanked the leash. But I pulled too hard, and Vinnie let out a choking gasp. Now people were getting mad. Was Mom's face turning beet-red, I wondered?

But I had to keep going: I needed to complete this requirement for the Pets Merit Badge.

In a final attempt, I yelled hoarsely, "Vinnie, HEEL!!!"

Vinnie sorrowfully dropped his head and began to pee all over himself. More pee than I'd ever seen!

People whispered behind their hands. I already knew it: my dog show was over. No sitting, no shaking, no staying, and definitely no speaking. All that practice wasted! I could kiss that first-place ribbon goodbye.

Well, I guess second place isn't that bad, right?

I knelt down beside Vinnie and stroked his back, saying gently, "Sorry, boy. So sorry." Relieved to have his master back in his right mind, Vinnie followed me out of the arena. I didn't have to give a command. For the next hour, Mom, Vinnie, and I plodded around the dog show, trying to blend in and forget the disaster. We waited for the award ceremony, thinking it would bring an end to this embarrassment.

Lesson learned #67:
I learned from Jesus' mother Mary, especially during her Son's trial and crucifixion, that a good parent always sticks by her kid, just as Mom stuck by me (even though I surely embarrassed her).

First Place Loser

With only two Gordon Setters competing, I psyched myself up for second prize. Clearly I wasn't going to take home first prize, but second place seemed OK — except the late, great NASCAR champion Dale Earnhardt opined, "Second place is just first place loser." Either way, a red ribbon to show my Scoutmaster and my buddies seemed like a face-saving merit.

First prize was announced. Joan and her Bridget walked to center stage to get their gold. Loud applause.

I waited breathlessly for the judge to declare me and Vinnie second-prize winners.

He announced gleefully, "Second prize goes to…"

My heart raced. I would grab my second-place ribbon and forget this miserable experience forever.

"...Joan and Bridget!"

WHAT?!!

Had my ears played a trick on me? No, but my pride sure had.

Joan and Bridget took the stage again!

It was a blur. I choked back tears and hoped people would think I was sweating in the July heat.

It hit me: **I had won third place of two dogs!**

Third place! In Dale Earnhardt's reckoning, that was second place loser. Or more like last place loser!

Talk about sheer rejection! No rejection since — not a prospective prom date, a friend, or a boss — has ever felt worse than that dog show rejection. Yet years later, God gave me so much joy in recounting this sad but silly story of wrecked teenage dreams. The joy comes because of all the lessons He taught me through that experience.

> ### Lesson learned #68:
> I now see that the more I am rejected, the more I lean into Jesus, and this leaning in grows my intimacy with Him.

We have all known the raw emotion that comes from being rejected. Rejection is no respecter of age: children, students, adults all feel its sting. And who more than Jesus?

> ### Lesson learned #69:
> Even when people seem to act cruelly, God guides us through all rejections, even bringing joy and often laughter later on.

Have you ever felt third place of two? Third place of one? Perpetually LAST place? Do you ever feel like you don't fit in? You are not alone. We've all felt that way at one time or another.

Even Jesus felt that way — especially Jesus. Rejection is a challenging but honing experience you'll share with Jesus on your Journey to Joy.

Your Journey to Joy

JOY CHALLENGE #7: Discover how you can know joy in rejection.

CHAPTER 7 QUESTIONS:

1. Why did Jesus allow Himself to be rejected?
2. Why have humans continued to reject God?
3. What did Jesus say about the world rejecting His followers? What are some examples of this?
4. Why is rejection so hard for us to take?
5. Which lesson was most helpful to you? Why?
6. How can you bring joy to someone who's facing rejection?

Jesus' Journey to Joy®

Chapter 8

Jesus knew joy because He anguished in pain.
(Matthew 27:46)

8

JOY IN PAIN

About three in the afternoon Jesus cried out in a loud voice, "Eli, Eli, lema sabachthani?" (which means "My God, my God, why have you forsaken me?"
Matthew 27:46 (NIV) (Jesus' fourth statement from the cross)

How can you know Me if you don't know pain?
~ The Holy Spirit

Jesus knew joy because He anguished in pain.

Jesus anguished

"Surely he took up our pain and bore our suffering, yet we considered him punished by God, stricken by him, and afflicted." Isaiah 53:3 (NIV)

Anguish is mental or physical pain or suffering. Jesus knew pain. Fully God and fully man, Jesus anguished in pain far beyond what we can imagine. When we consider Jesus' pain throughout His life, culminating on the cross, we could describe it this way: Jesus anguished.

Dr. C. Truman Davis medically details the anguish of the cross:

> Jesus experienced hours of limitless pain, cycles of twisting, joint-rending cramps, intermittent partial asphyxiation, searing pain where tissue is torn from His lacerated back as He moves up and down against the rough timber. Then another agony begins — a terrible crushing pain deep in the chest as the

pericardium slowly fills with serum and begins to compress the heart. One remembers again the 22nd Psalm, the 14th verse: "I am poured out like water, and all my bones are out of joint; my heart is like wax; it is melted in the midst of my bowels."

As we'll see, Jesus privately acknowledged His imminent suffering. But He also publicly responded to His pain in a number of ways that are highly instructive to us. Here are several examples.

What Jesus said about HIS pain

Throughout His earthly ministry, Jesus encountered pain, ranging from mental (public ridicule) to physical (the cross). And Jesus warned His disciples of the pain He would experience at the hands of the Jewish leadership.

> From that time on Jesus began to say plainly to his disciples that he must go to Jerusalem and suffer many things at the hands of the elders, the chief priests and the teachers of the law, and that he must be killed and on the third day be raised to life. Matthew 16:21 NIV

So how did Jesus respond to the high priest regarding His accusers? "Then the high priest stood up. He asked Jesus, 'Aren't you going to answer? What are these charges that these men are bringing against you?' But Jesus remained silent" (Matthew 26:62-63 NIRV).

Jesus remained silent — incredible!

Lesson learned #70:
In pain, sometimes our best option is to remain silent like Jesus did.

After the Sanhedrin sentenced Jesus to death for blasphemy, more pain ensued. "They all condemned him as worthy of death. Then some began to spit at him; they blindfolded him, struck him with their fists, and said, 'Prophesy!' And the guards took him and beat him" (Mark 14:64-65 NIVUK).

Pain and more pain. Again Jesus remained silent before His mocking accusers! In this response Isaiah's prophecy speaks loudly: "He was oppressed and afflicted, yet he did not open his mouth. Like a lamb led to the slaughter and like a sheep silent before her shearers, he did not open his mouth" (53:7 CSB).

Though He warned His disciples of His upcoming suffering, Jesus often remained silent before His tormentors, and He never complained.

Lesson learned #71:
Despite His pain, Jesus never complained. Remember, complaining kills joy and brings blame (Philippians 2:14-15).

Pilate sentenced Jesus to inhumane pain

At the hands of Pilate, the Roman governor of Judea, Jesus' pain escalated. I think John 19:1 (NIV) is among the Bible's most understated passages: "Then Pilate took Jesus and had him flogged."

We can say that sentence in one short breath. But that flogging would leave most of us breathless and probably lifeless. Those condemned to crucifixion often didn't survive the flogging beforehand. Jesus did, but at great cost.

> Then Pilate took Jesus and had Him flogged. The soldiers twisted together a crown of thorns and put it on His head, and dressed Him in a purple robe. And they went up to Him again and again, saying, "Hail, King of the Jews!" and slapping Him in the face (John 19:1-3 BSB).

If Pilate had any hopes that Jesus' brutal scourging would placate the Jewish leaders and Passover crowd, his next interaction with them revealed both his cowardice and his condemnation.

> "Here is your king," Pilate said to the Jews. But they shouted, "Take him away! Take him away! Crucify him!" "Shall I crucify your king?" Pilate asked. "We have no king but Caesar," the chief

priests answered. Finally Pilate handed him over to them to be crucified (John 19:14-16 NIV).

By now Jesus was approaching the ultimate earthly suffering He would face: crucifixion. We'll look at that in Chapter 11 Joy in Dying to Self.

Lesson learned #72:
God uses inhumane physical pain to work glorious results.

After Mel Gibson's *The Passion of the Christ* was released, Jim Caviezel, the actor who portrayed Christ, revealed in an interview on the *Today* show that "he dislocated his shoulder carrying the cross, caught pneumonia and a lung infection, [and] endured cuts, scrapes, and backaches from the chains he bore."

The interview also shed light on just how painful Jesus' scourging was.

> The scourging sequence is as agonizing to watch as the Crucifixion itself. Caviezel was chained to a post with a board behind him to absorb the blows. Gibson instructed the two actors inflicting the beating to hurl their lashes overhand as if throwing a baseball. Caviezel took a blow to his back when one of the actors aimed poorly. "It just extended over the board and hit me with such a velocity that I couldn't breathe," Caviezel said. "It's like getting the wind knocked out of you. The stinging is so horrific that you can't get air. I turned around and looked at the guy, and I tell you, I may be playing Jesus, but I felt like Satan at that moment. I turned to him, and a couple of expletives came out of my mouth." Moments later, Caviezel was struck again, the lash slicing the gash in his back.

Whether you've seen *The Passion of the Christ,* read the gospel narratives of Jesus' passion, or smacked your thumb with a hammer, we get a sense of the excruciating pain Jesus endured on Calvary's cross. His **fourth** saying there is a desperate cry close to his death: "About three in the afternoon Jesus cried out in a loud voice, *'Eli, Eli, lema sabachthani?'*

(which means 'My God, my God, why have you forsaken me?')" (Matthew 27:46 NIV).

And this is my point, a lesson seared in pain.

This is a sampling of Jesus' pain, but what about His disciples' pain?

Lesson learned #73:

As humans, we may understand a *fraction* of the pain Jesus endured, but we can *never* understand the SPIRITUAL pain that Jesus, our substitutionary Sacrifice, experienced when He bore, absorbed, and satisfied the Father's wrath for our sin (Galatians 3:13).

What Jesus said about His disciples' pain

Pain is what most of us try to avoid, but it is one of the places where our walk with Christ gets real. How do we walk through pain with Him?

Matthew's account of Jesus sending out His disciples (10:17-25) is a primer in understanding what Jesus said about the pain and persecution His disciples will suffer because of Him. "Beware of people, because they will hand you over to councils and flog you in their synagogues. And you will be brought before governors and kings because of me, as a witness to them and the Gentiles" (Matthew 10:17-18 NET).

True to form, Jesus didn't mince words, and He wasn't merely speculating on what His disciples *might* experience: persecution awaited them like a trap in plain view. And just as the disciples couldn't avoid their duty because of the fear of pain, so we can't be intimidated because of persecution, regardless of how dire our situation appears. MacDonald explains:

> They would be dragged before governors and kings for Christ's sake. But God's cause would triumph over man's evil. Man has his wickedness, but God has His way. In their hour of seeming defeat the disciples would have the incomparable privilege of

testifying before rulers and Gentiles. God would be working all things together for good.

Lesson learned #74:

When following Christ, pain is as unavoidable as the promise is sure that the Spirit of the Father will be speaking and working through us. God speaks through our pain.

The pain Jesus endured brought about the greatest joy we could ever know. We'll consider this in greater detail in Destination Joy? (Chapter 12). But for now, a story of unique pain and joy.

My Journey to Joy

We hate it.

We ignore it.

We even try to hide it, but we can't avoid it.

Pain. It comes in many forms: physical, emotional, mental, and spiritual to name a few.

We hardly need define it, because each of us already knows pain more closely than we ever wished. Pain is a four-letter-word, but so is love. It seems love and pain are inseparable, especially in the Biblical context. And that's the point of this chapter: how do we know joy in pain?

"Off the scale" pain

Early in my twenties, I developed something I thought only the elderly experienced: large hemorrhoids. Well, that's about the most awkward sentence I've ever written! Before you skip this story because you think you might get sick, please know that it is short on gory and long on glory. I'm amazed how God worked through the most physical pain I have ever experienced; any future physical pain could only *tie* it.

To keep the "wretch" factor low, I've borrowed a term my colorectal surgeon, Dr. Keeton, used to describe that area down there. I'll simply call it my "tailpipe." Sometimes the pain was so severe I thought I'd die: an 11...on a scale of 10. Similar to back pain, this type of tailpipe pain can't be relieved by sitting, standing, or sleeping: you can't escape it. After I limped through a decade of cyclic tailpipe issues and varying degrees of profound pain, it was clear: both the intensity and the frequency of my flare-ups were increasing. Only surgery would fix it.

Somehow, word of my pending tailpipe surgery got around. People were falling out of trees just to tell me how painful this surgery would be. The descriptions were all similar.

- "Oh, Travis, that tailpipe surgery REALLY hurts!" warned my grandfather.

- "I had that same lousy procedure, and it left me out of work for a month," recalled a neighbor.

- "My wife said I cried every day for weeks afterward," another friend confessed.

> ### Lesson learned #75:
> You're not alone in your pain. No matter what type of pain you're experiencing, there are likely other people you know who've also gone through it. Even in embarrassing types of pain, it's comforting to know that God isn't "singling you out."

My fear of such pain repeatedly drove me to my knees. "God, won't you PLEASE take away this pain? Can you hear me, God? Won't you take away this pain?" I set out to do my own internet research on alternatives to tailpipe surgery. There had to be another way, right?

An awkward assessment

Like a stray mongrel that refuses to leave you alone, so the awkwardness of my situation followed me to Dr. Keeton's office. My nurse, whom I'll call Sally, a soft-spoken, elderly woman, handed me a gown. "You'll need to fully undress and put this gown on so it opens in the back," she instructed as she pulled the privacy curtain around me.

Yep, I had expected that. So far so good.

When I was ready, Nurse Sally opened the curtain. To my horror, I saw something I'd missed at first: a strangely sloping table that peaked in the middle. It didn't take *any* imagination to see how this worked.

Nope. I hadn't expected that.

"Mr. Zimmerman," nurse Sally kindly instructed, "let's have you climb up on the table here, face down. I've been doing this a long time, and most people find this part is a little uncomfortable."

Unable to hide my flushed expression, I scaled the table and felt my face turn even redder as blood drained down to my face and feet on opposite sides of the peak. And there for all to see, my tailpipe rose high into air.

Awkwardness now gave way to dread.

Nurse Sally adjusted a bright light onto my tailpipe. "Now, this part won't hurt a bit, but I'm going to open up your gown, so that we can see what we're dealing with here." I wanted to crawl into the floor.

Facedown on the table, I felt her slowly draw back my gown and then quickly recoil in surprise, her shrill voice rising as if a swarm of angry hornets had unexpectedly stung her:

"Oh, GOOD HEAVENS, dear, that must HURT!!!"

I felt my face go even redder. Dr. Keeton, who had slipped in from behind, offered his own, slightly more composed and analytical assessment:

"Hmmm, yes, that *is* acute."

Did he really just use a word that sounded like "cute" while examining my tailpipe?

After the exam, I tried to convince Dr. Keeton of the alternatives to surgery that I had researched.

Dr. Keeton: Travis, TRAVIS! I *appreciate* what you're trying to do here; I really do. But none of these alternatives will work for you; your tailpipe issues are too big. What you need is a good old-fashioned hemorrhoidectomy. It's a proven procedure that's very effective. But it's going to hurt like heck.

Me: (*silence*)

Like a rat in a trap, I really began to worry about the massive pain that surely awaited me.

Lesson learned #76:
Despite our desire to sidestep it, sometimes God plans pain for us that we can't avoid, no matter how hard we try. But He'll teach us many lessons we probably wouldn't learn otherwise.

A power shower

Now faced with a brutal surgery and recovery, I felt God had boxed me in, leaving me no pain relief options. Desperate to avoid it, I cried out to Him, "God, would you PLEASE remove this pain from me!?"

Was God ignoring me?

The evening before my early morning procedure I took Dr. Keeton's advice to enjoy one last shower. I climbed into the steam and immediately renewed my desperate pleas.

"Lord, I really don't want to go through this pain. I've known it for over ten years now, and I can't bear to think of it getting worse. But, Jesus, I know You are a man of sorrows and familiar with pain and suffering. So, if more pain is something You want me to go through, I accept that as Your will, Lord. Amen."

At that very moment a change occurred in me. As comforting as the hot shower felt washing over me, the peace of God washing over me in that moment was even more comforting. As I reached for a towel, my eyes fixed on my cross necklace resting on the bathroom sink. The Holy Spirit gently whispered to me:

"How can you know Me if you don't know pain?"

Tears rushed down my face as I stared at my cross necklace and remembered what Jesus did on His cross. I had so focused on my own pain that I had forgotten all God had accomplished through His pain! And that through His pain God brought such joy!

Quietly, peacefully, and humbly I prayed, "God, come what may, I'm ready to experience even more pain for Your glory."

<u>Lesson learned #77:</u>
In times of doubt and worry, keep talking to God, keep reaching out to Him. While He may or may not whisper to you, His peace is always available as you seek Him with all your heart.

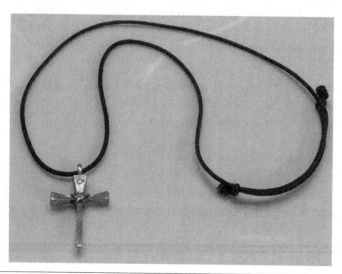

God calls through pain

Well, Dr. Keeton surgery pronounced my surgery "unremarkable" — truly a matter of perspective, right? And my prolonged recovery proved to be just as painful as advertised.

- **You make a grown man cry.** Recovery was so painful that I cried every day for weeks.

- **A busy intersection.** I made a short-lived decision to avoid eating — Dr. Keeton had deadpanned that tailpipe recovery was so difficult because it's a busy intersection. Not funny.

- **Bathed in pain.** Several times a day, I sat in steaming hot water in my wife's bathtub to deaden the pain. Her pink Women's Study Bible helped distract me. Cute, but I was desperate.

Two weeks into recovery, I was still in a lot of pain. "How much longer, Lord, how much longer?" I bawled.

And *that's* when the Holy Spirit spoke to me in an undeniable whisper and placed a calling on my life:

> ## "Travis, speak My Word, and I will take care of the rest...."

Suddenly muted, I opened Suzanne's Bible to my favorite Scriptures, Jesus' Sermon on the Mount. I quickly realized God was leading me to study, memorize, and speak His Word to others. God's call on my life was so clearly and simply presented to me, yet I suddenly got fearful. How could I even think that I could stand in front of anybody and speak Jesus' words verbatim — it seemed impossible to me!

Speaking God's Word is a very humbling proposition, but I've built my entire adult life upon Him, the Living Word, the Rock of my salvation (Psalm 89:26). In 2009, in obedience to His call, Suzanne and I founded Speak My Word Ministries, which in 2016 became A Faithful Dad. It's been the adventure of a lifetime!

Lesson learned #78:

God's call upon my life came through my life's most intense physical pain! What unbridled joy God brings through even our most painful times!

Jesus knew joy in pain.

Your Journey to Joy

JOY CHALLENGE #8: Share how you can know joy in pain.

CHAPTER 8 QUESTIONS:

1. What did Jesus say about His pain?
2. What did Jesus say about His disciples' pain?
3. What's the most pain you've experienced? How did you handle it?
4. Which lesson was most helpful to you? Why?
5. What lessons did God teach you through your pain?
6. How can you bring joy to someone who's suffering in pain?

Psalms of Joy

When the LORD restored the captives of Zion,
we were like dreamers.

Then our mouths were filled with laughter
and our tongues with shouts of joy.
Then it was proclaimed among the nations,
"The LORD has done great things for them."

The LORD has done great things for us;
we are filled with joy.

Restore our captives, O LORD,
like streams in the Negev.

Those who sow in tears
will reap with shouts of joy.

He who goes out weeping,
bearing a trail of seed,
will surely return with shouts of joy,
carrying sheaves of grain.

Psalm 126:1-6 BSB

Jesus' Journey to Joy®

Chapter 9

Jesus knew joy because He thirsted in sickness.
(John 19:28)

9

JOY IN SICKNESS

Later, knowing that everything had now been finished, and so that Scripture would be fulfilled, Jesus said, "I am thirsty."
John 19:28 (NIV) (Jesus' fifth statement from the cross)

Health is not valued till sickness comes.
~ Thomas Fuller

> ## Jesus knew joy because He thirsted in sickness.

Jesus thirsted

An unnatural sickness descended on Jesus' body as He contorted on the cross in the early afternoon of Good Friday. His gruesome ordeal was almost at an end, His body nearly spent. Dr. C. Truman Davis describes what happened medically speaking:

> It is now almost over. The loss of tissue fluids has reached a critical level; the compressed heart is struggling to pump heavy, thick, sluggish blood into the tissue; the tortured lungs are making a frantic effort to gasp in small gulps of air. The markedly dehydrated tissues send their flood of stimuli to the brain."

He gasped His **fifth** cry, "I thirst."

In His cry, we keenly sense Jesus' humanity. But while His broken body thirsted for water (He twice refused drink), the thirst to do His Father's will was far greater. Throughout His earthly walk Jesus encountered sick and thirsty people who desired to know the Messiah. And to be blunt, *not* knowing Jesus is far worse than any sickness: it's why Jesus endured Calvary. Here are three examples of sick and thirsty people whom He encountered.

A sick woman thirsts for healing

A large crowd followed and pressed round him. And a woman was there who had been subject to bleeding for twelve years. She had suffered a great deal under the care of many doctors and had spent all she had, yet instead of getting better she grew worse. When she heard about Jesus, she came up behind him in the crowd and touched his cloak, because she thought, "If I just touch his clothes, I will be healed." Immediately her bleeding stopped and she felt in her body that she was freed from her suffering. Mark 5:24-29 (NIVUK)

Broke, hurting, and out of options, this longsuffering woman displayed the faith of a child in trusting that healing could be hers if only she could just reach out and touch His cloak. Jesus affirms her in Mark 5:34 (NIV): "Daughter, your faith has healed you. Go in peace and be freed from your suffering."

It is faith in Christ that brings us through sickness, lack, and hurt, no matter how long the ordeal ahead or behind us is. We can emulate this dear woman's longsuffering faith, which Christ rewarded. And as we know all too well, sometimes God chooses to heal us, and sometimes He doesn't.

<u>Lesson learned #79:</u>

Rejoice in Him in times that God heals us, but trust in Him in times that He doesn't.

Mark records the woman's glorious healing: "Immediately her bleeding stopped and she felt in her body that she was freed from her suffering"

(5:29 NIV UK). Yet I also see a more subtle, parallel lesson to what would come shortly in Jesus' seventh and final cry from the cross…

Lesson learned #80:

Just before Jesus died, His bleeding stopped — because His heart was close to stopping — and He felt in His body that He was freed from suffering, uttering, "Father, into Your hands I commit My spirit."

Jesus' Journey to Joy would soon be complete.

Here's the second story of a sick and thirsty person: the woman at the well.

A Samaritan woman thirsts to know Messiah

Jews and Samaritans were as oil to water: the Jews disdained the Samaritans. So, Jesus' dialogue with a Samaritan woman, "sick" from her lifestyle choices and thirsting for salvation, is especially intriguing. Ignorant of Jesus' true identity, this Samaritan woman's initial curiosity led to a deeper discussion that could quench any thirst.

> The woman said, "I am surprised that you ask me for a drink. You are a Jew and I am a Samaritan." (Jews are not friends with Samaritans.) Jesus said, "You don't know what God gives. And you don't know who asked you for a drink. If you knew, you would have asked me, and I would have given you living water." The woman said, "Sir, where will you get that living water? The well is very deep, and you have nothing to get water with. Are you greater than Jacob, our father? Jacob is the one who gave us this well. He drank from it himself. Also, his sons and flocks drank from this well." Jesus answered, "Every person who drinks this water will be thirsty again. But whoever drinks the water I give will never be thirsty again. The water I give will become a spring of water flowing inside him. It will give him eternal life." John 4:9-14 (ICB)

The woman at the well represents many of us: we talk about our dry-mouth thirst, which, of course, God relieves in His own time. But He has so much more for us: living water that can quench *any* thirst forever!

- We peer through a narrow straw, but God *sees* in all dimensions: full color, full sound, and full glory.

- We sip through a narrow straw, but God *floods* us with His love: greater than even Niagara Falls!

Lesson learned #81:

Why settle for a meager straw when you can go straight to the abundant Source of living water!

We learn later in the narrative of John 4:39 (ESV) that, "Many Samaritans from that town believed in him because of the woman's testimony, 'He told me all that I ever did.'" Are we sharing our testimony of Christ's faithfulness with thirsty people?

I find it so humbling, so awe-inspiring that Jesus, Lord of living water, willingly went through such suffering, such sickness, such thirst, so that we could have life everlasting. The next lesson is a testament to God's faithfulness to His children.

Lesson learned #82:

Jesus allowed the ground beneath the cross to drink His blood, so that we — sick with sin — might drink the living water that wells up to eternal life! We will never "thirst" again!

Now we return to the narrative of Jesus and Lazarus in John 11 for our third story of sick and thirsty people. Let's first see how Jesus desired to heal all the sick, then look in particular at the story of Lazarus.

Not all sickness leads to death

On the cross, Jesus refused His own human needs (thirst, pain, blood loss). However, Scripture shows how Jesus satisfied the needs of so many before He was crucified. "Then Jesus went to all the towns and villages, teaching in their synagogues, preaching the good news of the kingdom, and healing every disease and every sickness" (Matthew 9:35 HCSB).

In one prominent example, His friend Lazarus, the brother of Mary and Martha, was deathly ill. Knowing Jesus' heart and ability to heal the sick, Mary and Martha told Jesus, "Lord, the one you love is sick."

After learning that her brother had died, Martha thirsted to understand why Jesus hadn't saved him. She mourned, "Lord, if only you had been here, my brother would not have died" (John 11:21 NLT).

Jesus' earlier answer to His disciples would prove so promising: "But when Jesus heard about it he said, 'Lazarus's sickness will not end in death. No, it happened for the glory of God so that the Son of God will receive glory from this'" (John 11:4 NLT).

So, Jesus raising Lazarus from the grave not only brought great benefit to Lazarus, Mary, and Martha, but more importantly, it glorified God, and in turn Jesus would be glorified through it. In fact, just one chapter later Jesus speaks of the Father glorifying Him in death.

> Now My soul has become troubled; and what shall I say, "Father, save Me from this hour"? But for this purpose I came to this hour. Father, glorify Your name. Then a voice came out of heaven: "I have both glorified it, and will glorify it again." John 12:27-28 (NASB)

The love, courage, and faithfulness Jesus demonstrated in obedience to the Father produces another amazing lesson.

Lesson learned #83:

In healing Lazarus' sickness, which glorified God, Jesus previewed His own sickness of thirst and death on the cross — His glorification, which the Father had promised!

My Journey to Joy

All of us have experienced sickness of some kind; most of us have probably stayed home from school or work at one time or another. But sometimes sickness can pass from a trivial trial to a faith-shaking, near-death experience. My dear friend, Darren Carson, experienced just that.

My "brotha from anotha motha"

Ever meet someone you just "clicked" with right away? That's what happened when I met Darren "DC" Carson, my "brotha from anotha motha." A co-worker called us that because DC and I got along so well. We relished the name.

I first met DC in late 2005 when we worked together. In his first week on the job, DC asked me a provocative series of questions over lunch:

DC: TZ, how tall are you?

TZ: (*confused*) Uh, 5'11". Why?

DC: 5'11" – yes. Then why are you walking around this place like you're 5'5"?

TZ: (*even more confused*) What do you mean?

DC: What I mean, TZ, is that God made you 5'11" and He gave you great skills to use for His glory. Yet you're walking around this place like you're 5'5", scared of your own shadow, all stooped over. Now, don't overcorrect that situation and start walking around on your tippy toes like you're 6'2" or something. Walk around like you're 5'11" just as God made you. And smile!

TZ: (*swallowing hard*) You've got a point, DC.

And with that, we both busted out laughing until we cried!

Lesson learned #84:
Even when work wearies us, God can encourage us through our closest friends to remind us of the joy we have in Him!

DC and I enjoyed hundreds of those laughing lunches together. So given our close relationship, you can imagine how upset I was when my brotha got sick. Very sick.

Facing death, feeling peace

A couple of years after we started working together, DC grappled with an increasing number of debilitating health issues, including diabetes, poor circulation, and congenital heart failure. In late 2007, God led DC and his bride, Regina, to North Carolina. Despite the distance, our brotherhood grew closer. Meanwhile, DC grew much, much sicker. The primary cause was that two vital organs — his heart and his kidneys — were failing. All needed to be replaced.

Wasting no time, Regina got DC to Duke University Hospital, where the doctors connected him to life support while he awaited a double organ transplant. As you would expect, it is rare for both a heart and a kidney to be available. Each time we talked, DC tried to keep it light. But he also talked about how many deceased transplant patients on his hospital floor had been wheeled past his room, patients who weren't able to hold out long enough for a transplant. Though DC stayed strong, Regina and I were unnerved. We never voiced it, but we both wondered, would DC survive?

The first day DC was admitted to the hospital, he called me. I was shocked.

DC: TZ, I just wanted to tell you that I love you.

TZ: I love you, too, DC. Everything OK?

DC: I'm good, TZ. We called the family in. I had one last chance to hug and kiss my wife, my kids, and my grandkids. And now I'm calling you to say my goodbyes. There's a pretty good chance my body won't survive this procedure.

TZ: (*on the verge of tears, trying to stay strong*) Oh, no...oh, no....

DC: (*beaming*) It's OK, TZ, God's totally got this! Whether He keeps me here or not, I accept His will. I'm ready to see Him face to face, ready to see my mom again. Just pray for Regina, the kids, and me, OK? TZ, God's got this!

It was unmistakable: here, staring death in the face, DC had life! I could spot it hundreds of miles away.

I ended our call with a whimper, collapsed on my bed, and bawled my eyes out. "God," I whispered, "please don't take DC yet. His family needs him! But, Lord, just like DC, I accept Your perfect will. Please give me the same peace You've given DC, Your peace. We trust You in this, Jesus. Amen."

Lesson learned #85:

Paul talks in Philippians 4:7 about "the peace of God that passes all understanding." For the first time in my life, I understood such peace, seeing it in DC even as he faced death.

A Joyful Reunion

Only God could have arranged this timing: a few weeks later my entire family was driving past Duke University Hospital on a Florida trip to visit grandparents. We all jumped at the chance to see DC and Regina.

As we pulled into the visitor parking, my heart churned with questions.

- Would God save DC?

- Would Regina be OK?

- How would our reunion be after not seeing each other for 5 years?

Minutes later, the elevator opened to DC's floor, and we seven Zimmermans spilled into the hallway as the nurse vectored us to DC's room. What happened next is pure, unadulterated joy!

The moment DC and I saw each other, we openly wept and laughed aloud. Unbounded joy! We embraced in beautiful brotherhood, overjoyed by this glorious homecoming God gifted to us. This picture of us visually captures that joy, but no image could describe the joy God gave us through this trial!

"Brothas from anotha motha"

Just before we parted, we hugged each other again — but more tightly than ever before. It turns out we both harbored the same troubling question: Am I seeing my brotha for the last time?

Lesson learned #86:

In our joyous reunion, despite the grave uncertainty, God blessed us with a tiny glimpse into what heaven might be like: meeting Jesus face-to-face, tears of joy, smiles of those we love most!

God's timing is perfect

After DC endured over 100 days in ICU and two gut-wrenching false alarms over failed potential donors (I'd never heard him so depressed),

God brought a double donor match for DC! And God's style showcases His perfect timing:

- February 12: DC received a new heart

- February 13: DC received a new kidney

- February 14, Valentine's Day: Regina got her husband back with a new heart (and kidney)!

- February 22, DC's birthday: Duke discharged DC and he returned home!

The sweetest aspect of this story: God isn't finished with DC yet!

Lesson learned #87:
Our God worked a glorious miracle amidst direst sickness. Don't trust your eyes or your experience, but trust the One who can save you!

Your Journey to Joy

JOY CHALLENGE #9: Talk about how you can know joy in sickness.

CHAPTER 9 QUESTIONS:
1. What's the longest you've ever been sick? Briefly, how did you get so sick?
2. How can we "Rejoice in Him in times God heals us, but trust Him in times He doesn't"?
3. Many Samaritans believed in Jesus because of the testimony of the woman at the well. How can you share your testimony of the Living Water? With whom can you share it?
4. Which lesson was most helpful to you? Why?
5. How can you know joy when someone you love experiences sickness?
6. How can you bring joy to someone who's suffering now in sickness?

Psalms of Joy

I give you thanks, O Lord, with all my heart;
I will sing your praises before the gods.

I bow before your holy Temple as I worship.
I praise your name for your unfailing love and faithfulness;
for your promises are backed by all the honor of your name.

As soon as I pray, you answer me; you encourage me by
giving me strength.

Every king in all the earth will thank you, Lord, for all of them
will hear your words.

Yes, they will sing about the Lord's ways,
for the glory of the Lord is very great.

Though the Lord is great, he cares for the humble
but he keeps his distance from the proud.

Though I am surrounded by troubles,
you will protect me from the anger of my enemies.
You reach out your hand,
and the power of your right hand saves me.

The Lord will work out his plans for my life—
for your faithful love, O Lord, endures forever.
Don't abandon me, for you made me.

Psalm 138:1-8 NLT

Jesus' Journey to Joy®

Chapter 10

Jesus knew joy because He cried out in misery.
(John 19:30)

10

JOY IN MISERY

When he had received the drink, Jesus said, "It is finished." With that, he bowed his head and gave up his spirit.
        John 19:30 (NIV) (Jesus' sixth statement from the cross)

Any discussion of how pain and suffering fit into God's scheme ultimately leads back to the cross.
        ~Philip Yancey

Jesus knew joy because He cried out in misery.

A fitting finish

As defined by Google dictionary, misery is "a state or feeling of great distress or discomfort of mind or body." We could say Jesus' crucifixion was a state AND feeling of great distress AND discomfort of mind AND body AND soul. Toward the end of His crucifixion, Jesus was literally almost beyond misery.

Dr. C. Truman Davis explains:

> The body of Jesus is now in extremes, and He can feel the chill of death creeping through His tissues. This realization brings out His **sixth** cry, possibly little more than a tortured whisper: "It is finished." His mission of atonement has completed. Finally, He can allow His body to die.

Here, beyond the overwhelming agony of crucifixion, there is a much greater joy in what is to come: Jesus has completed His atoning work. By the apostle James's definition, His pure joy of trials is nearly over; He has persevered through the world's most difficult trial. Like a marathoner staggering across the finish line, Jesus' joy of completing the race was in sight. He cried out in misery: "When he had received the drink, Jesus said, 'It is finished.' With that, he bowed his head and gave up his spirit" (John 19:30 NIV).

Now, I confess that me trying to empathize with Jesus' crucifixion is similar to me trying to empathize with my bride's pregnancies. But because Suzanne delivered five kids, I can at least:

- Describe some of her highlights and challenges over the total of ~50 months she was pregnant;

- Wince with her pain as the contractions came on strong; and

- Cry and rejoice when each baby was born.

But to say I *know* what she went through being pregnant — not happening. Similarly, having read the gospel accounts and watched *The Passion of the Christ*, I can certainly describe Christ's crucifixion. But I could never say I know what He went through. Who of us can, really?

What we can see is that Jesus fully relied on the Father; this was not a misery of despair or hopelessness then. No, this was a misery of His earthly body paying the price for our sins. Those who were present could certainly see the tip of that iceberg of misery — the pain and torture He suffered on the cross. But the real core of Jesus' suffering — the massive, unseen root of the iceberg — was the price He paid for our sins. We can never see that sacrifice, yet we all benefited from it.

> ### Lesson learned #88:
> As wracked with pain and near to death as He was, Jesus knew joy as He was completing His atoning work. It is much greater than the joy of a supreme marathoner crossing the finish line.

In a flashback just before His passion, Jesus also experienced misery as He mourned the Holy City's unwillingness to obey God.

Lament of Jerusalem

Even as Jesus approached the cross, He didn't give up on Jerusalem. He expressed His passion and sorrow: "O Jerusalem, Jerusalem, the city that kills the prophets and stones those who are sent to it! How often would I have gathered your children together as a hen gathers her brood under her wings, and you were not willing!" Luke 13:34 (ESV)

On the one hand: As God, Jesus knows the joy that awaits those who would submit to His authority, those who would choose Him. He wants the best for His children.

On the other hand: Jesus knew His love for them would be a saving love. But in rejecting Him, they were exchanging the joy that comes from obedience for the destruction that comes from disobedience. Parents also experience misery when their kids won't listen to wisdom but instead make poor choices with predictable, often tragic results. These poor choices include:

• Crossing the street without looking both ways

• Playing video games instead of studying

• Using illegal drugs, among many others.

How much more does our Father God want the best for us? After all, He made us and knows us inside and out!

Lesson learned #89:
Jesus wept over Jerusalem's stubbornness to obey God. Disobeying Jesus doesn't lead to joy, it leads to destruction.

Jesus also knew the dire judgment the Romans would soon inflict upon the Holy City.

Jesus weeps over Jerusalem

Now as Jesus approached Jerusalem just before His passion, He cried out for her inhabitants, knowing the joy they were bypassing and the judgment they would face.

> And when he drew near and saw the city, he wept over it, saying, "Would that you, even you, had known on this day the things that make for peace! But now they are hidden from your eyes. For the days will come upon you, when your enemies will set up a barricade around you and surround you and hem you in on every side and tear you down to the ground, you and your children within you. And they will not leave one stone upon another in you, because you did not know the time of your visitation." Luke 19:41-44 (ESV)

First-century Romano-Jewish scholar Josephus describes the Roman horrors of Jesus' warning:

> When they went in numbers into the lanes of the city with their swords drawn, they slew those whom they overtook without and set fire to the houses whither the Jews were fled, and burnt every soul in them, and laid waste a great many of the rest; and when they were come to the houses to plunder them, they found in them entire families of dead men, and the upper rooms full of dead corpses, that is, of such as died by the famine; they then stood in a horror at this sight, and went out without touching anything. But although they had this commiseration for such as were destroyed in that manner, yet had they not the same for those that were still alive, but they ran every one through whom they met with, and obstructed the very lanes with their dead bodies, and made the whole city run down with blood, to such a degree indeed that the fire of many of the houses was quenched with these men's blood. *The Wars of the Jews*, 6:8:5

According to Josephus, 1.1 million non-combatants died in Jerusalem in AD 70, mainly as a result of the violence and famine. Many of the casualties were observant Jews from across the world, such as Babylon and Egypt, and who had travelled to Jerusalem to celebrate the yearly Passover. Instead they were trapped in the chaotic siege.

God's discipline is similar to a parent warning a misbehaving child of his imminent punishment, "This is going to hurt me more than it's going to hurt you." The punishment causes misery, because sin carries a price that must be paid. But discipline also ultimately brings joy: "My child, pay attention when the Lord disciplines you. Don't give up when he corrects you. The Lord disciplines everyone he loves. He severely disciplines everyone he accepts as his child" (Hebrews 12:5-6 GW).

Lesson learned #90:
God's discipline is sown in misery but reaped in righteousness.

Pass through but don't remain!

Not only did Jesus foresee how the Romans would destroy Jerusalem, He also foresaw Satan desiring to destroy the lives of men and women everywhere. In other words, He knew the misery Satan had in store for the disobedient, namely us. Satan often disguises disobedience as something beneficial and desirable (as Eve found the apple desirable in Genesis 3). Even two thousand years later, a modern band, The Soup Dragons, suggest this in their lyrics: "I'm free to do what I want any old time." Yet as we know too well, the consequences of Adam and Eve's disobedience continue to reverberate today.

At the beginning of this chapter, I offered a dictionary definition of misery. But God's Word puts misery in personal terms that we can all understand. Here are some of Scripture's most chilling accounts of misery.

- "Then [God] will say also to those on the left hand, 'Depart from me, you cursed, into the everlasting fire which is prepared for the devil and his angels.'" Matthew 24:41 (NHEB)

- "...where their worm does not die and the fire is not quenched." Mark 9:48 (ESV)

- "And the devil, who deceived them, was thrown into the lake of burning sulfur, where the beast and the false prophet had been thrown. They will be tormented day and night for ever and ever." Revelation 20:10 (NIV)

"Wait a minute!" you might say. "These passages are describing hell!"

Indeed – that's my point. Hell *is* misery.

At its heart, God's wrath and judgment are hell — pure misery. If we *remain* in misery, we remain in hell. And who wants to remain with "that ancient serpent, who is the 'devil', or Satan" (Revelation 20:2)?

Nobody.

But let's flip the question around: Is misery hell?

No.

Misery is a tool God uses to make us more like Him.

"How can God use misery, much less produce joy from it?" we might ask. God doesn't waste experiences, and misery is no exception. God uses misery for His glory (Romans 8:28) to bring about joy, and He *certainly* doesn't stay in misery.

Here's the connection.

God allows trials to enter our lives, and they often involve misery. Knowing this, when we enter into misery with Christ, we can be assured we will ultimately leave misery behind, because He does NOT remain in misery. Sure, God will extract from misery valuable attributes like patience and perseverance; and we can be confident that we will pass through misery *with* Him.

> ### Lesson learned #91:
> In our deepest suffering, we can cry out in our misery, as Christ cried out on the cross. And we can do so knowing that Jesus passes through with us — that's pure joy!

The stories I share from my journey have much misery but an even greater harvest of joy.

My Journey to Joy

A Perfect Storm

There's a direct correlation: the more trials, the more misery. And of course, the real prospect for more joy! In the year before my Dad died, God blessed us with these simultaneous trials, a perfect storm:

- My wife, Suzanne, was tested for cancer; the physician team called the suspicious tissue "a mass".

- Dad's frontotemporal dementia worsened to the point where we had to institutionalize him.

- Mom's cancer wasn't going away, but instead progressing.

- One of our sons was tested for a brain tumor due to his peculiar behavior.

- I was tested for bone cancer and working part-time jobs (with no benefits).

At this point, Suzanne, though concerned, took all these things in stride. I, however, was beginning to unravel. When I lost my full-time job about a year earlier, I rudely discovered I had been stuffing my feelings by ignoring these issues instead of relying on God.

Big mistake.

Lesson learned #92:

A perfect storm stole not only my job, but also my joy. God taught me to rely on Him more heavily, laying my big (and small) problems at His feet.

This next story is a humbling lesson He taught me: to trust Him through both good times and misery-filled trials.

Heretical advice?

It was a Saturday morning, the day of our son Trey's birthday. We had planned a backyard pool party. Normally, I love kids, cake, and hanging out, but on this day, I was in a thinly disguised foul mood. Then one Trey's best buddies accidently sprayed me with a hose. Much to my own surprise, I snapped at him, "STOP IT!!!"

This poor boy looked as surprised as if he had been slapped: Mr. Zimmerman — scout leader, soccer coach, and Sunday School teacher — yelled at him! Dropping the hose, he scampered to the safety of his mom who, like all the other moms, was gasping at me in horror. Especially my wife. I was doubly embarrassed, totally red-faced.

I had really stepped in it, so I decided to step inside for the rest of the party.

The following Tuesday morning was my men's Bible study, which also served as an accountability group of 10 men. I was the youngest by about 40 years. Clearly, my snapping at Trey's friend was an accountability issue that I needed to share with my group. So I did. Harvey, 83 at the time, had some great advice.

Me: Fellas, I really messed up.

Harvey: *(ominously)* What did you do?

Me: *(frowning, head down)* I yelled at my son's best friend, totally freaked him out.

After I briefly shared the story with the men, Harvey spoke up again.

Harvey: (*kindly*) Oh, Travis, you weren't angry with that little boy.

Me: (*confused*) I wasn't?

Harvey: No, you're angry with God.

Me: (*really confused*) I am?

Harvey: Yes, and you just need to go have it out with God.

Me: (*indignant*) That's heresy, Harvey.

Harvey: (*compassionately*) Oh, Travis, God has big shoulders, He can take it.

Me: (*determined*) I'm not going to do that, Harvey.

Harvey: OK, I understand, but will you do one thing for me?

Me: (*guarded*) What's that?

And then Harvey pulled a fast one on me! Shrewder than an "I triple-dog dare you" taunt, Harvey had the *audacity* to ask me this...

Harvey: (*smiling*) Will you pray about it?

Me: Yeah, I'll pray about it...but I'm NOT going to do it, Harvey!

And then I ducked out before I could further embarrass myself. Here's the lesson I was to learn.

Lesson learned #93:

God never says, "Wow! I didn't see *that* coming!" He already knows what you're thinking, so out with it!

Having it out with God

I continued spiraling downward, although I prayed as I had promised Harvey I would. But there was just no way I was going to "have it out with God." No way.

Until about two weeks later.

Suzanne flew to Albuquerque for a class reunion, so I was in charge of all five kids. That Sunday I awoke in a miserable mood. Though I didn't recognize it at the time, I was angry at God over our trials, just like Harvey said. We drove to church. After settling the kids in their Sunday school classrooms, I muttered under my breath, "God and I are going to have it out; I'm going to give Him a piece of my mind." I drove to a nearby empty parking lot: just God and me in the hot July sun.

But my boiling temper was even hotter than that July day.
Finally, I had had enough. I had it out with God.

I literally screamed at the top of my lungs, "I'M SICK OF THIS!!! WHY ARE YOU PUTTING ME THROUGH THIS!!! I HATE THIS!!!"

I yelled so loud in my minivan (windows closed, of course) that my ears rang from the volume of my screams.

I cried out again, "WHY ARE YOU DOING THIS TO ME? I'M IN THE CLUB! I wear Your cross, I read and memorize Your Word, I bring people to know You, I speak Your Word. WHY ARE YOU DOING THIS TO ME? WHAT KIND OF RECRUITING IS THIS?!! Why would ANYBODY want to be a Christian if this is the way YOU treat those who follow YOU? What kind of recruiting is this?!!"

"GOD, WHAT KIND OF RECRUITING IS THIS?!!"

Exhausted and boxed in, I burst into tears of absolute frustration, crying for almost 10 minutes. Between sobs, I was just waiting for God to say something — anything! And you know what He told me?

NOTHING!

"Fine!" I whispered testily between sobs, "Have it your way!"

After I cried myself out, I tried composing myself but found it hard to camouflage all the tears that had landed on my khaki slacks. I drove back to church to retrieve my kids, and I was irritated that so many people were looking at me. Fine, here, nothing to see: move along!

That evening Suzanne flew home. But she started having an allergic reaction to one of her meds and had to go straight from the airport to the ER!

"Perfect, just PERFECT! This is EXACTLY what I'm talking about, God! What kind of recruiting is this?!"

But then I came around to reason. And three days later, as I was on my knees, asking God to forgive me for my temper tantrum, I heard the still, quiet voice of the LORD whispering to me:

> **"You keep asking me, 'What kind of recruiting is this?' Here's My answer: because, Travis, if you can go through trials like this (sick wife and son, dying dad and mom, no job) and *still* proclaim Me, that's GREAT recruiting."**

I was shocked. I opened my eyes…and started to cry again, but this time they were tears of joy. Spotting a pattern?

God also brought Matthew 11:6, one of my favorite Scriptures, to mind: "Blessed is the one who does not fall away on account of Me." Through my tears, I smiled to myself over His perfect timing.

Like Jesus, we can know joy, because we cry out to God in our misery!

> ### Lesson learned #94:
> "Because if you can go through trials like this and *still* proclaim Me, that's GREAT recruiting!"

Little did I know then that these "perfect storm" trials were like a dress rehearsal to a seven-year nightmare that God had in store for us just one year later. Put simply, it was my most challenging trial to my faith, my family, and my life. Though it literally almost killed four of us, it taught us all the most important lesson of all: the joy of dying to self. Yet that is NOTHING compared to how Jesus died to self.

Your Journey to Joy

JOY CHALLENGE #10: Expand on how you can know joy by crying out in misery.

CHAPTER 10 QUESTIONS:
1. Why was Jesus willing to endure the misery of the cross?
2. "Misery is a tool God uses to make us more like Him." How so?
3. To what degree has misery been a part of your trials?
4. Why do we blame God when we find ourselves in trials?
5. Which lesson was most helpful to you? Why?
6. How can you minister to someone who's experiencing misery?

PART 4

VICTORIOUS JOY!

I consider that our present sufferings are not worth comparing
with the glory that will be revealed in us.
Romans 8:18 (NIV)

Rejoice, rejoice, O Christian! Lift up your voice and sing
Eternal hallelujahs to Jesus Christ, the King!
The Hope of all who seek Him, the Help of all who find,
None other is so loving, so good and kind.

He lives (He lives), He lives (He lives), Christ Jesus lives today!
He walks with me and talks with me
Along life's narrow way.
He lives (He lives), He lives (He lives), salvation to impart!
You ask me how I know He lives?
He lives within my heart.
~ Alfred H. Ackley, He Lives

Jesus' Journey to Joy®

Chapter 11

Jesus knew joy because He died to self.
(Luke 23:46)

11

JOY IN DYING TO SELF

Jesus called out with a loud voice, "Father, into your hands I commit my spirit."
When he had said this, he breathed his last.
     Luke 23:46 (NIV) (Jesus' seventh statement from the cross)

The core of the gospel is found in the work of Jesus Christ. Especially in the death of
Christ on the cross, God's righteousness is revealed – a righteous hatred of sin and a
righteous commitment to his covenant promise to bring blessing to the world.
    ~ Evangelical Convictions

Jesus knew joy because He died to self.

What is dying to self?

Leonard Bernstein, the late conductor of the New York Philharmonic
Orchestra, was once asked to name the most difficult instrument to play.
Without hesitation, he replied: "The second fiddle. I can get plenty of
first violinists, but to find someone who can play the second fiddle with
enthusiasm — that's a problem; and if we have no second fiddle, we
have no harmony."

Hit close to home? It seems we all want to play first fiddle. But we should
follow Christ's example — even He yielded. Jesus played second fiddle
to the Father in perfect harmony with the Spirit.

Jesus knew joy, because He died to self.

In short, dying to self is the essence of the Christian life: taking up our cross and following Christ. He taught this in Luke 9:23-24 (EHV): "If anyone wants to come after me, let him deny himself, take up his cross daily, and follow me. For whoever wants to save his life will lose it, but whoever loses his life for my sake will save it."

In fact, Jesus says we *can't* be His disciples *without* following Him: "And if you do not carry your own cross and follow me, you cannot be my disciple" (Luke 14:27 NLT).

But who really wants to die? Here's a response to that: as it turns out, we're already dead! As the apostle Paul soberly reminds us in Ephesians 2:1 (NASB), "And you were dead in your trespasses and sins...."

Whether you're a Christian or not, you are a dead man walking if you don't carry your cross and follow Jesus each day. Those who don't know Christ journey through their lives, only to step off a cliff at the end of it all. For those who would know Christ, we must pick up our cross — and by doing so, find true life. So God is asking you to choose between two types of death:

1. a death that leads to oblivion (stepping off a cliff), or
2. a death that leads to life — dying to self!

Which will it be?

Know this: His death leads to true life. Jesus promises this in John 10:10 (ESV): "The thief comes only to steal and kill and destroy. I came that they may have life and have it abundantly."

MacDonald explains this further:

> The Lord Jesus does not come to the human for any selfish reason. He comes to give, not to get. He comes that people may have life, and that they may have it more abundantly. We receive life the moment we accept Him as our Savior. After we are saved, however, we find that there are various degrees of enjoyment in

this life. The more we turn ourselves over to the Holy Spirit, the more we enjoy the life that has been given to us. We not only have life then, but we have it more abundantly.

Again, there is no greater enjoyment in this life than knowing Christ. Though it's simple to remember but hardly simple to live out, I've found this Sunday School acronym helpful in recalling my priorities: To have joy, remember J.O.Y.

1.   (J)esus – first
2.   (O)thers – second
3.   (Y)ou – last

Lived out, it's a restatement of the two most important commandments: love God and love others. God probably won't ask you to literally die for Him, especially on a cross, but He will ask you every day — multiple times a day — to die to self.

Lesson learned #95:

Whoever loses his life for Christ will save it. We can have a full life, a J.O.Y.ful life by dying to self.

Know Jesus, know joy

In a dispute with His opponents, Jesus plainly revealed that His obedience to the Father necessitated dying to Himself — specifically through a torturous death upon the cross.

> So he said to them, "You will lift up the Son of Man. Then you will know that I AM. You will know that whatever I do is not by my own authority. You will know that I say only what the Father has taught me. The one who sent me is with me. I always do what pleases him. So he has not left me alone." While he was saying these things, many people believed in him.
> John 8:28-30 (ERV)

Jesus *always* does what pleases the Father. His action and this Scripture passage relate directly to this guide's main premise: **Joy is KNOWING JESUS, following Him through all our trials.**

Lesson learned #96:

Dying to self pleases the Father. We are dependent upon Him: on His love, His mercy, His grace, His protection, His will. There can be no greater joy!

One death, many lives

In explaining to the festival attenders how He would die, Jesus used a farming illustration to help His audience understand the critical nature of dying to self: "I tell you the truth, unless a kernel of wheat is planted in the soil and dies, it remains alone. But its death will produce many new kernels — a plentiful harvest of new lives" John 12:24 (NLT).

And let's call this what it is: a miracle of new lives, joy everlasting! But Jesus would know this joy only through the cross and death. Burge notes,

> Jesus recognizes the culmination of all he has been attempting in Judaism. The cross and death are all that remain. But…it is not a death of disgrace and shame; Jesus will be glorified and this will mysteriously result in great things. The same is true of his followers. Self-effacement and denial are the only pathways of finding the company of Jesus or the honor of the Father.

Burge acknowledges the pathway of self-effacement and denial. Through that we can readily see the journey laid out before us, a journey to joy (Hebrews 12:2).

Lesson learned #97:

Jesus walks with us on this path of dying to self, because He did so Himself.

That's so amazing! A commentator for the *NIV Life Application Study Bible* writes,

> This is a beautiful picture of the necessary sacrifice of Jesus. Unless a kernel of wheat is buried in the ground, it will not become a blade of wheat producing many more seeds. Jesus had to die to pay the penalty for our sin, but also to show his power over death. His resurrection proves he has eternal life. Because Jesus is God, Jesus can give this same eternal life to all who believe in him.

Lesson learned #98:
Not only do you save your life by dying to self, but also more lives will be saved by Christ's multiplicative work, because you have surrendered your own life to Him.

Dying to self leads to rejoicing

Jesus instructed His disciples in the Upper Room just before His arrest. There He reminds them of the previous conversations He'd had with them about Him going away. That had initially saddened them: "You have heard me tell you, 'I'm going away, but I'm coming back to you.' If you loved me, you would rejoice that I'm going to the Father, because the Father is greater than I am" (John 14:28 ISV).

Here we see Jesus submitting to the Father — dying to self — in obedience to His plans. Jesus would 'go away', but He would return days later, just as He promised. A key point here is that His going away — His death — is cause for us to rejoice. His pain, our gain! His death, our life! His life, our joy!

Jesus continues in John 14:29-31 (NCV).

> I have told you this now, before it happens, so that when it happens, you will believe. I will not talk with you much longer, because the ruler of this world is coming. He has no power over

me, but the world must know that I love the Father, so I do exactly what the Father told me to do.

Lesson learned #99:
Jesus not only defeated death, but He defeated the enemy, the prince of this world. Sweet victory in Jesus!

As He got to the heart of the matter in the Upper Room, He taught one of His greatest lessons. "Greater love has no one than this: to lay down one's life for one's friends" (John 15:13 NIVUK).

Physical death is the ultimate example of dying to self! Jesus perfectly obeyed Father God by submitting to death.

> Who, being in very nature God, did not consider equality with God something to be used to his own advantage; rather, he made himself nothing by taking the very nature of a servant, being made in human likeness. And being found in appearance as a man, he humbled himself by becoming obedient to death — even death on a cross! Philippians 2:6-8 (NIV)

And, finally, the moment arrived. The beating, the torture, the anguish, the suffering done in 3, 2, 1....

Last breath before death

"Father, into your hands I commit my spirit" (Luke 23:46 NIV) — Jesus' seventh and final cry from the cross!

Dr. C. Truman Davis concludes, "With one last surge of strength, He once again presses His torn feet against the nail, straightens His legs, takes a deeper breath, and utters His **seventh** and last cry, 'Father! Into thy hands I commit my spirit.'"

His final cry and ultimate submission — passing from life to death. He lived His entire life for the Father, in obedience to Him, and even in His last breath, He died in perfect submission to the Father.

Here Jesus was echoing Psalm 31:5, where the writer makes an announcement, not a request. Bromiley notes that traditionally this passage is called "The Word of Reunion," which theologians interpret to be the prophecy of Jesus joining God the Father in Heaven.

Hamilton has written that:

> When darkness seems to prevail in life, it takes faith even to talk to God, even if it is to complain to him. These last words of Jesus from the cross show his absolute trust in God: "Father, into your hands I commit my spirit." This has been termed a model of prayer for everyone when afraid, sick, or facing one's own death. It says in effect: "I commit myself to you, O God. In my living and in my dying, in the good times and in the bad, whatever I am and have, I place in your hands, O God, for your safekeeping."

Lesson learned #100:
In dying to self, in complete obedience to the Father, Jesus ensured not only His joy but ours as well!

Almost as a formality, Pilate's men confirmed Jesus' death. "But when they came to Jesus and found that he was already dead, they did not break his legs. Instead, one of the soldiers pierced Jesus' side with a spear, bringing a sudden flow of blood and water" (John 19:33-34 NIV).

The initial result of dying to self?

Christ is DEAD!

Was joy gone, never to return?

My Journey to Joy

A Horrific Fall

Simply put, this was the most difficult section for me to write for reasons that will soon be obvious.

I had no idea how pivotal Wednesday, October 19, 2011 would be for our family.

We had just celebrated our 17th wedding anniversary, Suzanne had just completed her first half marathon with all six of us cheering her at the finish line, and my brother (and business partner) Eric and I were enjoying the best sales quarter of our company's 18-year history. All was right with the world!

Just as Eric and I were grabbing lunch between frenetic sales calls, my phone rang: Suzanne.

Hastily swallowing my food to take the call, I heard Suzanne crying out in a way I'd never heard before: in sheer terror. "Trav, I slipped and fell down wet stairs! I'm in so much pain that I can't move, I can't get up! I need your help!!!"

I soon learned that Suzanne landed with such force that both of her shoes flew off her feet, and she was unable to move for close to a half hour. We also learned a lot more. Initially, Suzanne suffered:

- A fractured sacrum (the bone above the tailbone)

- A micro fractured pelvis

- A 95% labral tear in her hip joint, and

- A ruptured vertebrae

Her horrific fall essentially put her body into shock, which began an onslaught of subsequent medical issues. Suzanne's rapidly declining health was like a cartoon where one character is wearing an ugly Christmas sweater that has a snag at the bottom. Grabbing hold of the snag, another character starts to pull the snag, and the whole sweater unravels from the bottom to the top, one row at a time.

Except this was no cartoon: it was a nightmare. Summarizing, Suzanne:

- Was bedridden for 14 months, able only to sleep, eat, and homeschool our kids;

- Underwent 13 surgeries in 3 years;

- Visited the ER around 40 times for pain and related issues;

- Endured almost constant and often debilitating pain for over 6 years;

- Saw dozens of physicians, surgeons, and specialists who tried to address her pain; and

- Nearly died twice due to medical complications.

The severity of Suzanne's medical issues affected every aspect of our lives: our marriage, our relationship with our kids, our friends (many left us), our work, and our finances (we nearly went bankrupt again).

The worst part of it all? I witnessed my bride cry out in pain and writhe in miserable contortions, unable to find relief. Torture for her. Agony for us. I often cried myself to sleep, desperately wondering why God was allowing my bride and our family to suffer so much. I fought to know joy, but it was a titanic struggle.

Lesson learned #101:

Sometimes God allows us to suffer for years, and joy seems elusive. It's in those times that we must cling to Him with everything we've got and trust Him.

As I mentioned in Chapter 6, Joy in the Death of a Loved One, I return now to the early morning of Mom's death, because during this time God taught some life-changing lessons through us dying to self.

The early morning of Mom's death revisited

12:02 am, Thursday, July 24, 2014.

Couldn't sleep, kept thinking about the unsettling events of the past week.

For the third time in 2014, Suzanne and Mom were hospitalized concurrently, twice at the *same* hospital. This would be the third and last time for Mom. She had texted me, "Must be tough to have both of us here. Tough indeed. I'm praying for you."

Earlier in the week, Suzanne's surgeon had admitted her for an emergency procedure to stem her 10-out of-10 pain. The first procedure failed, so she endured two more emergency procedures within three days that left her temporarily wheelchair bound. Yet, in between those two procedures, God worked a gentle miracle through my bride.

Though Suzanne and Mom were on separate floors, my recovering bride — smarting from the pain of her first surgery — knew she needed to check on her mom-in-law. Amazingly, Suzanne slid herself into a wheelchair, took the elevator to Mom's floor, and slowly wheeled herself to Mom's room. She took in Mom's emaciated frame and, as only a mother could know, Suzanne knew what she needed to do.

Determined, Suzanne forced herself up out of her wheelchair and drew warm water into a portable basin. Placing the basin on a stand, she struck a precarious balance by holding Mom's bed rail in one hand while using the other to dip a small sponge into the warm water. She wrung the sponge out and gently sponge bathed my dying mother's head and face.

Over the next several minutes, despite her pain, Suzanne lovingly washed Mom — her head, then her arms and hands, and then her legs. Lastly, Suzanne washed Mom's feet, just as Jesus washed His disciples' feet (John 13:5). When she finished, Suzanne collapsed into her wheelchair. She was discharged later that day, only to return for a second emergency procedure the next day. She made Jesus proud.

Lesson learned #102:

Even in moments encumbered by sorrow and pain, God can work such tender miracles for His glory. Despite the obvious challenges, Suzanne counts this moment as one of her most precious memories with her mother-in-law: joy in a time of dying.

Finally, I drifted off to sleep.

12:53 am, Thursday, July 24, 2014.

Even though I was anticipating it, Eric's call startled me. I quickly went from an uneasy sleep to a sickly semi-consciousness and fumbled in the dark for my phone.

"I'm sorry to tell you the news, Travis, but Mom passed at 12:10 this morning."

Sadness. Relief. Loneliness.

The phone call didn't surprise Suzanne: pain robbed her of sleep.

"I've got to go see Mom," Suzanne announced.

"Honey, you just got home last night after two emergency surgeries in three days," I pleaded. "Shouldn't you recover first?"

"NO! I've GOT to see her!" she wailed.

No choice: Suzanne was committed. We made the short drive back to the hospital. Suzanne could only walk a few steps, so I dropped her off at the front of the hospital, settling her into a wheelchair to ease her discomfort. I drove off into the darkness to find a parking spot.

Yet, as I drove, I couldn't shake this from my mind. Over the past several years, Suzanne wanted me to go to her medical appointments. Mom wanted me to go to her medical appointments. Our kids wanted me to be at every event. With my jobs and taking care of the house, I just couldn't do it all! "I'm doing a lousy job as a husband, a lousy job as a son, and a lousy job as a dad!" I exclaimed into the blackness.

Parking in a remote visitor's lot, I sprinted back to meet Suzanne. Winded, I wheeled her through the hospital entrance as a dark thought stormed into my mind.

"It's 1:30 a.m., and here I am wheeling my disabled wife up to see my dead mother. Is this *suffering* all that You have for me, God?!"

Lesson learned #103:

God taught me that I truly had to die to myself if I wanted to live for Him. It's the same for you. He didn't intend for us to do everything by ourselves. God wants us to die to self!

In retrospect, that moment of wheeling Suzanne to my mother's hospital room is seared in my brain. It was like a snapshot that captured and summed up all the trials we had been through in the preceding ten years.

At the time I felt only exasperation, but now I sense relief. He is sovereign!

Knowing Jesus

The days after Mom passed were challenging, even though we were relieved that she no longer suffered. With Suzanne's pain, Dad's and Mom's deaths, declining finances, and plummeting morale, we kept crying out to the Lord, asking Him to help us make sense of what we were experiencing as a family.

Again I thought, is this *suffering* all that You have for me, God?!

And just when I least expected it, God surprised me in a glorious way, in a way that only He could do. Early one morning, when I am most attentive to His prompting, the Lord reminded me of my desperate cry over 10 years earlier after seeing *The Passion of the Christ*: **Jesus, I just want to _know_ You!**

In fact, in the cacophony of joys, trials, celebrations, and suffering, I'd forgotten my humble request from a decade ago. Yet God is faithful! In the middle of my morning quiet time, He conclusively answered my theatre exit request.

"Travis, you asked to *know* Me more closely, and I've answered your prayer through <u>suffering</u>."

Wow. Wow. Wow.

The Spirit immediately led me to the apostle Paul's teaching in Philippians 3:10-11 (NIV): "I want to know Christ — yes, to know the power of his resurrection and participation in his sufferings, becoming like him in his death, and so, somehow, attaining to the resurrection from the dead."

I closed my Bible and closed my eyes in prayer. I hadn't expected it, but God had responded to the most desperate cry of my heart, teaching me so many lessons in following Him that I would have never learned otherwise.

Lesson learned #104:
Joy is *knowing* Jesus, following Him through all your trials!

Your Journey to Joy

JOY CHALLENGE #11: Choose one way you can die to self and how you'll go about it.

CHAPTER 11 QUESTIONS:
1. What did Jesus accomplish in dying on the cross? Why did He do that?
2. What does Jesus mean in Luke 14:27 that we cannot be His disciples if we don't carry our cross and follow Him?
3. Why is it so hard to die to self?
4. What's one thing you've sensed the Holy Spirit nudge you to do in order to die to self? Did you obey? What were the results?
5. How easy or difficult is it to challenge someone to die to self? How would you go about it?
6. Which lesson was most helpful to you? Why?

Jesus' Journey to Joy®

Chapter 12

Jesus knew joy because He conquered death!
(Hebrews 12:2)

12

DESTINATION JOY?

Let us fix our eyes on Jesus, the pioneer and perfecter of our faith, who for the joy set before Him endured the cross, scorning its shame, and sat down at the right hand of the throne of God.
Hebrews 12:2 (NIV)

Quickly now go tell the world;
Christ, the Lord, He is risen;
the power of God forever raised Him from the grave.
~ Jeremy Riddle, Christ is Risen

Jesus knew joy because He conquered death!

Jesus' Journey to Joy is complete!

We know that Christ, who was brought back to life, will never die again. Death no longer has any power over him.
Romans 6:9 (GWT)

Christ's climactic journey is complete, just as Isaiah predicted in Isaiah 53:11 (NIV): "After he has suffered, he will see the light of life and be satisfied…."

Christ's suffering has produced His ascension, just as He repeatedly promised His disciples. "The Son of Man is going to be delivered into the hands of men, and they will kill him. And when he is killed, after three days he will rise" (Mark 9:31 ESV).

The culmination of His journey to joy is upon us! In Romans 6:9 (GWT) the apostle Paul celebrates Christ's conquering death, because He "will never die again. Death no longer has any power over him."

So many thought that joy had been extinguished by Jesus' death. But for those who would follow Him in His suffering, His very death brings new life — a tremendous joy! The writer of Hebrews celebrated His victory in 12:2 (NIV):

Let us fix our eyes on Jesus, the pioneer and perfecter of our faith, who for the joy set before Him endured the cross, scorning its shame, and sat down at the right hand of the throne of God.

Yes, Jesus knew the cross's torment, shame, and death, but He also knew the joy set before Him by conquering death. Climatically, here's the massive outcome: **Jesus' Journey to Joy is complete!**

<u>Lesson learned #105:</u>
We can know His joy by not only fixing our eyes on Jesus but following Him with our cross to reach His shared joy!

The news of the completion of Jesus' Journey to Joy, before it was shared with anyone else, was revealed first to the unlikeliest person....

Rejoicing with an unlikely witness

God's Word is so full of joy, but arguably no more intimately joyful than in the account of Jesus appearing to Mary Magdalene. Mark 16:9 tells us she is the first to see our resurrected Jesus. The apostle John recounts what happens next:

> Now Mary stood outside the tomb crying. As she wept, she bent over to look into the tomb and saw two angels in white, seated where Jesus' body had been, one at the head and the other at the foot. They asked her, "Woman, why are you crying?"

"They have taken my Lord away," she said, "and I don't know where they have put him." At this, she turned around and saw Jesus standing there, but she did not realize that it was Jesus.

He asked her, "Woman, why are you crying? Who is it you are looking for?"

Thinking he was the gardener, she said, "Sir, if you have carried him away, tell me where you have put him, and I will get him."

Jesus said to her, "Mary."

She turned toward him and cried out in Aramaic, "Rabboni!" (which means "Teacher"). Jesus said, "Do not hold on to me, for I have not yet ascended to the Father. Go instead to my brothers and tell them, 'I am ascending to my Father and your Father, to my God and your God.'"

Mary Magdalene went to the disciples with the news: "I have seen the Lord!" And she told them that he had said these things to her. John 20:11-18 (NIV)

Glorious tears of joy! Put yourself in Mary's sandals: she's alone, confused, and grief-stricken. She's wondering, "Where is Jesus? Has this gardener carried Him away?"

Recognizing her fragile state, Jesus softly calls her by name, by her *first* name!

"Mary."

Mary is *overjoyed*! Christ is risen!

Can you imagine that? Unbridled joy!

But here's the thing: Jesus didn't call just Mary. He calls each one of us — whether we're joyful or sad, confused or clear-headed, alone or among people — by our *first* name, too. "He calls his own sheep by name and leads them out" (John 10:3 NIV).

"Gianna."

"Charlie."

"Susan."

"(insert your name here)."

> ### Lesson learned #106:
> The risen Christ offers eternal life by calling each of us by name. There is no greater joy than knowing Jesus!

And what makes this first appearance of the risen Christ even more remarkable is that Jesus once again does the unexpected, at least in the world's eyes. Rather than first appearing to the powerful (Caesar, Pilate, the Sanhedrin) or to His disciples (Peter, James, John), Jesus first appeared to an unlikely witness: a woman! Fantastic!

R.B. Edwards notes, "In a society in which women were not counted as full members of a congregation and were discouraged from studying the law, Jesus taught women alongside men (Matthew 14:21, 15:38, etc.)."

Jesus appeared first to a woman. How much He teaches us through this!

> ### Lesson learned #107:
> Jesus' teachings, His life, and His joy are for all people!

Mary Magdalene obediently shared Jesus' message with His disciples.

Rejoicing with His disciples

Mary Magdalene wasn't the only one afraid that Jesus' journey had plunged to a bitter end. The disciples feared the worst, too. But Jesus appeared among them to calm their raging fears and dispel their nagging doubts.

On the evening of that first day of the week, when the disciples were together, with the doors locked for fear of the Jewish leaders, Jesus came and stood among them and said, "Peace be with you!" After he said this, he showed them his hands and side. The disciples were overjoyed when they saw the Lord.
John 20:19-20 (NIV)

In His greeting, "Peace be with you!" we sense the jubilance in His voice. Scripture clearly articulates that the disciples were "overjoyed when they saw the Lord." But does this prove that Jesus had joy Himself at this moment?

Of course it does!

Joy comes only from God. We can't limit God, so neither can we limit His joy! The disciples were overjoyed, and that joy came from Jesus: He is simply radiant!

Lesson learned #108:
Jesus' joy is infectious!

Rejoicing in His return

There is no doubt that Jesus' first coming produced joy beyond measure. And He promises to come back soon! His assurance in Mark 13:26 (BSB) is, "Then they will see the Son of Man coming in the clouds with great power and glory."

His great power conquered death, but He will also, in God's perfect timing, conquer *all* evil. The apostle John beautifully records the results of evil's defeat in Revelation 21:3-4 (ERV):

> I heard a loud voice from the throne. It said, "Now God's home is with people. He will live with them. They will be his people. God himself will be with them and will be their God. He will wipe away every tear from their eyes. There will be no more death, sadness, crying, or pain. All the old ways are gone."

But, at this writing, that time is not yet; it is still to come. We needn't look far to know that evil is still very much present, active, and menacing. The apostle Peter brings everything back to suffering — a primary reason I wrote this guide — in 1 Peter 4:19 (NIV): "So then, those who suffer according to God's will should commit themselves to their faithful Creator and continue to do good."

We, as followers of the risen, conquering Christ, should always commit to our "faithful Creator and continue to do good." That commitment, my friends, is perseverance.

Lesson learned #109:
Consider it pure joy, my brothers and sisters, whenever you face trials of many kinds, because you know that the testing of your faith produces perseverance. James 1:2-3 (NIV)

My Journey to Joy

Destination Joy?

Through this guide, and through our lives, we've walked with Jesus on His journey. That journey included good times, transitions, rejection, and dying to self, to name a few. Jesus, considering the joy set before Him (Hebrews 12:2), endured the cross, and His journey has reached its final destination. Jesus' journey is complete.

But what about our journey? Will *we* also reach destination joy here on earth?

No!

As we've seen, joy is not something we get once for all or someplace that we arrive and are done! Joy is a way of life. Even the Pharisees struggled with this in Luke 17:20-21 (NIV):

> Once, on being asked by the Pharisees when the kingdom of God would come, Jesus replied, "The coming of the kingdom of

God is not something that can be observed, nor will people say, 'Here it is,' or 'There it is,' because the kingdom of God is in your midst."

It seems the Pharisees were looking for a temporal sign, a political upheaval, or a powerful outward show, but this is not what Jesus intended then or now. And if we're honest with ourselves, aren't we sometimes like the Pharisees?

Jesus again claimed that the kingdom of God — Himself! — was in their presence. It's not a *place* you *get* to, but an ongoing relationship you *have* with God!

In a sense, God's kingdom is already but not yet. GotQuestions? explains, "Believers are actively taking part in the kingdom of God, although the kingdom will not reach its full expression until sometime in the future. We are 'already' in the kingdom, but we do 'not yet' see it in its glory." Thankfully, Christ's saving work on the cross is sufficient and finished, but Christ will return again to completely vanquish evil. It is an evil with which each of us will struggle. In the meantime, even as He was leaving them to go to the cross, Christ promised His disciples, "I will ask the Father, and He will give you another Helper, that He may be with you forever" (John 14:16 NASB).

Lesson learned #110:

No matter how painful your trials are, no matter how long your earthly journey seems, God will be with you forever. He will never leave you!

And not only is His presence with us, calming our hearts in the direst trials, but He also lives with us and walks *with* us *through* those trials. This is clear even in His name, Immanuel: God with us. "Since we live by the Spirit, let us walk in step with the Spirit" (Galatians 5:25 BSB).

Again, the walk Paul speaks of is simply another way of depicting a journey to the Way! Paul relates that progression by relating it to the sufferings we all walk through.

Not only that, but we also rejoice in our sufferings, because we know that suffering produces perseverance; perseverance, character; and character, hope. And hope does not disappoint us, because God has poured out His love into our hearts through the Holy Spirit, whom He has given us. Romans 5:3-5 (BSB)

Do you see the progression Paul maps out here in our Journey to Joy?

Suffering → Perseverance→ Character → Hope = No disappointment = JOY!

Again, I offer, it's the journey with Jesus — not just the destination — that is so glorious.

Praise be to the God and Father of our Lord Jesus Christ! In his great mercy he has given us new birth into a living hope through the resurrection of Jesus Christ from the dead, and into an inheritance that can never perish, spoil or fade. This inheritance is kept in heaven for you. 1 Peter 1:3-4 (NIV)

Still, *is* there a destination and an end result of our faith?

Joyfully, yes! The apostle Peter reminds us of God's promise in 1 Peter 1:8-9 (NIV): "Though you have not seen him, you love him; and even though you do not see him now, you believe in him and are filled with an inexpressible and glorious joy, for you are receiving the end result of your faith, the salvation of your souls."

And the glorious salvation of our souls — fashioned through our relationship with Jesus in persevering through all our trials — will quite literally be Christ's crowning achievement in our lives!

Blessed is the one who perseveres under trial because, having stood the test, that person will receive the crown of life that the Lord has promised to those who love him. James 1:12 (NIV)

> ## Lesson learned #111:
> Christ assures our crown of life. Salvation is ours!

But even while we won't reach our final destination of joy here on earth, God gives us so much love, hope, and learning. The next story demonstrates this.

How God conquered my biggest fear

This story first appeared as a monthly update we sent out to our ministry supporters; the feedback was so overwhelming that I've included it here. Jesus found joy because He conquered death. I found joy because Jesus conquered my biggest fear.

Consider it pure joy, my brothers and sisters, whenever you face trials of many kinds, because you know that the testing of your faith produces perseverance. James 1:2-3 (NIV)

Have you "heard" from God lately?

People frequently ask me this question, or some version of it, and my answer is always the same: while others "hear" from God in worship, prayer, meditation, or through other people, etc., I "hear" from God most often when I'm reading the Bible, God's Word. It's a sure-fire way to better understand His love, mercy, and forgiveness, and, of course, His rescue plan. That's one reason why it's so important to be in His Word daily.

Aside from Bible reading, I also frequently hear from the Holy Spirit in my prayers. It's not an audible voice, but a thought or an idea that certainly didn't originate from my linear, often twisted thinking. And because I can't trust my motives, I *always* take what I have heard and compare it to the Bible, since the Holy Spirit will *never* contradict God's Word.

But occasionally God will just "talk" to me about something when I'm in the middle of doing nothing particularly spiritual: mowing the lawn, exercising, doing dishes, getting a shower. This particular instance was a Friday evening, August 18, 2017. As I was simply getting ready for bed, God revealed to me what I now regard as my life's most vital lesson, over a decade in the making. I was startled that this lesson involved my biggest fear: my paralyzing fear of loss.

God revealed to me that, over this past decade, He carried me through all of my life's worst losses including...

- Nearly losing my bride, Suzanne, to medical issues;

- Losing Dad and Mom, both at age 63, to horrific diseases;

- Almost losing one of my kids to depression caused by medical issues;

- Losing my last two grandparents;

- Losing jobs;

- Losing several friendships because of our medical issues and circumstances;

- Almost losing our house twice to bankruptcy;

- Losing most of our retirement savings; and

- Almost losing my own life to depression.

As my losses mounted over the years, I repeatedly asked — too frequently demanded — of Him, **"God, why are you doing this TO me?!"**

Not surprisingly, no answer ever came. Fine.

But this time God showed me the error of my repetitive question's perspective. So, I quietly rephrased it into a better question concerning my losses...

"God, why are you doing this FOR me?"

And this time, on this night, God absolutely humbled me as He answered that question...

> "Over this past decade, Travis, I guided you through all of your life's biggest fears to show you that you can always trust Me."

Amazing! That is truly the most impactful lesson He's ever taught me: God conquered my biggest fears — my fear of loss — to show me that I can always trust Him!

God did that *not* because He hates me, but because He loves me SO much that He sent His Son, Jesus, to die for me. This past decade has clearly been about dying to myself and having life in Him through perseverance developed during trials (James 1:2-3), even as He carried me. So now I can say, "Take what You will from me, Lord," because I especially know from these past ten years that no one or no thing will ever take my Jesus: I will never lose Him! Earthly loss has no permanent hold on me! And it has no permanent hold on you, either!

Lesson learned #112:
Knowing this, are you willing to allow God to conquer YOUR biggest fears?

See Afterword for a striking example of how God used this lesson!

Finally, I conclude this chapter with a joyous image God shared with me even as I was writing this guide.

Overflowing Joy

Eventually, our destination will culminate in His presence, where we will serve Him joyfully! "Better a day in Your courts than a thousand anywhere else. I would rather be at the door of the house of my God than to live in the tents of wicked people." (Psalm 84:10 HCSB). To better describe the story He's given me to share, let me first set it up with an analogy that depicts my finite — very finite — mind.

I've never been accused of being a visionary: I tend to be happy with my surroundings, live within my means, and shy away from too much change. In short, I guess you could call me accepting of situations.

By way of practical example, to the right of our kitchen stove, my wife keeps a small pottery jar that houses cooking utensils like spatulas, tongs, and wooden spoons. Through the years, as we added more kids, we naturally added more spatulas, more tongs, and more wooden spoons. In doubling our utensils, we had difficulty jamming all those utensils into that small pottery jar. Over capacity!

Occasionally while doing dishes I'd grumble under my breath about how challenging it was to get all those utensils into that little jar. I finally found that if I removed them all and straightened them up by tamping them down like a ream of paper, I could *barely* fit them all back into the jar. Good luck getting any of them out again!

Imagine my surprise when, one day, I saw Suzanne had bought a new, larger mouthed jar with plenty of room to spare for all our utensils!

Whoa, who knew?! That's the kind of "accepting situations" guy I am!

So now that I've set up the backstory to this beautiful picture God presented me, can I just say this? I can't WAIT to meet Jesus face to face!

Have you ever thought about that? If not, Mercy Me *totally* "stuck the landing" in describing what that first face-to-face encounter with Jesus might be like.

Surrounded by Your glory
What will my heart feel?
Will I dance for You, Jesus, or in awe of You be still?
Will I stand in Your presence or to my knees will I fall?
Will I sing Hallelujah?
Will I be able to speak at all?
I can only imagine.
I can only imagine.
"I Can Only Imagine" by Mercy Me

It is the moment I daydream about, the most joyous meeting of all! No, I'm not ready to meet Him any sooner than He's ready to bring me to His side, but one thing I know: meeting Jesus will be PERFECT! I can only imagine!

But then, as I started to think about seeing Dad and Mom again, my very finite mind got in the way.

- Meeting Jesus in heaven will be PERFECT!

- But will meeting Jesus *with* Dad (fully restored) be PERFECT-ER?

- And will meeting Jesus, and Dad, *with* Mom (fully restored) be PERFECT-ER-EST?

I get lost in the comparative and superlative adjectives: it blows my mind! Literally, for years, I'd been asking myself this question: How can you add to perfection?

To use a math analogy, it's like I kept dividing by zero — I blew up my brain!

Later, mercifully, the Holy Spirit provided glorious insight here.

God showed me that I had been thinking of joy and perfection in finite, human terms. For example, how can a full glass become fuller without overflowing? Or to put a fine point on it: How can I jam more utensils into our small pottery jar? In answer, the Spirit led me to Jesus' assuring words in John 15:11 (NLT): "I have told you these things so that you will be filled with my joy. Yes, your joy will overflow!"

So, now catch how God showed me His ways.

- When I meet Jesus, my joy glass — my pottery utensil jar — will be overflowing.

- Then when I meet Jesus *with* Dad, an even *bigger* cup of joy will be overflowing.

- And then when I meet Jesus and Dad *with* Mom, an even BIGGER cup of joy will be overflowing!

And, in His glorious presence, we will have such joy in celebrating Jesus with a cup of joy bigger than the world has ever known! It's surely part of the image the apostle Paul celebrates in 1 Corinthians 2:9 (GWT): "No eye has seen, no ear has heard, and no mind has imagined the things that God has prepared for those who love him."

Lesson learned #113:

There can be no greater joy than Jesus: unbounded, unimaginable, and unending!

Your Journey to Joy: Destination Joy?

JOY CHALLENGE #12: How can *you* know joy in all circumstances? Share your answer with a friend.

CHAPTER 12 QUESTIONS:

1. How does knowing that Jesus' Journey to Joy is complete encourage you in your Journey to Joy?
2. Why was it so significant that Jesus first appeared to Mary Magdalene?
3. Why does death have no power over those who follow Christ?
4. Which lesson was most helpful to you? Why?
5. Why will we not reach destination joy here on earth?
6. Knowing what you know, are you willing to allow God to conquer YOUR biggest fears? How so?

PART 5

REVIEW AND CONCLUSION

Therefore God exalted him to the highest place
and gave him the name that is above every name,
that at the name of Jesus every knee should bow,
in heaven and on earth and under the earth,
and every tongue acknowledge that Jesus Christ is Lord,
to the glory of God the Father.
Philippians 1:9-11 (NIV)

Jesus' Journey to Joy®

Let us fix our eyes on Jesus, the pioneer and perfecter of our faith,
who for the joy set before Him endured the cross, scorning its shame,
and sat down at the right hand of the throne of God.
Hebrews 12:2 (NIV)

JESUS KNEW JOY, BECAUSE...

Chapter	ACTION	TRIAL	SCRIPTURE
1	He MODELED ...	joy.	Matt.11:28-30
2	He CELEBRATED ...	in good times.	John 2:1-2
3	He PROVIDED ...	through His daily work.	John 4:34
4	He PRAYED ...	in transitions.	Luke 22:41-42
5	He FORGAVE ...	in relationships.	Luke 23:34
6	He PROMISED...	in the death of a loved one.	Luke 23:38-43
7	He PLANNED ...	for rejection.	John 19:26-27
8	He ANGUISHED ...	in pain.	Matt. 27:46
9	He THIRSTED ...	in sickness.	John 19:28
10	He CRIED OUT ...	in misery.	John 19:30
11	He DIED ...	to self.	Luke 23:46
12	He CONQUERED...	death!	Hebrews 12:2

13

REVIEW

Consider it pure joy, my brothers and sisters, whenever you face trials of many kinds, because you know that the testing of your faith produces perseverance.
James 1:2-3 (NIV)

Adversity is always unexpected and unwelcomed. It is an intruder and a thief, and yet in the hands of God, adversity becomes the means through which His supernatural power is demonstrated.
~ Charles Stanley

We've traveled Jesus' Journey to Joy by laying the foundation, considered joy through both outer and inner trials, and celebrated His victorious joy. This chapter reviews His journey and the final chapter concludes our guide.

PART 1 LAYING THE FOUNDATION

CHAPTER 1 THE REASON FOR JOY

Jesus knew joy, because He modeled joy. We opened up our discussion by introducing a story about a journey to joy. Well, actually, three stories: Jesus' journey, my journey, and your journey. We reflected on how great it would be to know joy through every station of life's journey, which led to our key question.

Key Question: How can I know joy in all circumstances?

Our key question helped us consider a good working definition for joy. According to the Evangelical Dictionary, joy is "a delight in life that runs deeper than pain or pleasure. From a Biblical perspective it is not limited by nor solely tied to external circumstances. Joy is a gift of God, and like all of his other inner gifts it can be experienced even in the midst of extremely difficult circumstances." And we introduced the premise.

Premise: Joy is knowing Jesus, following Him through all our trials.

We agreed that joy is learning from Jesus, it is taking up our cross and following Him daily, and it is found throughout God's Word. Jesus has many lessons for us; He is the reason for joy. We also introduced this guide's key verse.

Key Verse: "Consider it pure joy, my brothers and sisters, whenever you face trials of many kinds, because you know that the testing of your faith produces perseverance." James 1:2-3 (NIV)

After a short discussion of trials we encounter, we briefly considered joy vs. happiness and the simultaneous (aka "bittersweet") emotions that we all encounter in various situations.

Lastly, we overviewed Jesus' Journey to Joy, my Journey to Joy, and asked you to reflect on your Journey to Joy.

CHAPTER 2 JOY IN GOOD TIMES
Jesus knew joy, because He celebrated in good times. We suggested that celebrations are a wonderful aspect of God's kingdom, noting that Jesus' first recorded miracle occurred at a wedding. God's creation of the world was joy-filled, and we saw joy demonstrated in Jesus' baptism and anticipated when God banishes evil forever.

A beautiful lesson we learned is that Jesus is most joyous when we turn from death to life: every time a person receives Christ and His new life, all heaven rejoices!

We also learned that good times can indeed be trials if we expect only to encounter good times and never bad times. And our hearts can become proud in good times because we can forget God and even attribute our good times to our own doing.

Lastly, we considered our life's best moment ever, and joyously learned that our time with Jesus in heaven will be a zillion times better than our life's best moment on earth! Good times indeed!

PART 2 JOY THROUGH OUTER TRIALS

CHAPTER 3 JOY IN DAILY WORK

Jesus knew joy, because He provided through His daily work. Not only did Jesus preach the good news, but He was also a hard worker who helped provide for His family. Our work for God is of critical importance to Him, and God is looking for us to open ourselves up to do His will. That work is never easy, and many powerful people will try to oppose us at both work in the marketplace and work for His kingdom. Despite how busy He was, Jesus, Whom we should model, always took time to commune quietly with the Father.

In the end, though, Jesus came to do His Father's work. "My food," said Jesus, "is to do the will of him who sent me and to finish his work" (John 4:34 NIV). And that work was providing salvation, the goal of our faith. We also discussed dream jobs, "meh" jobs, and miserable jobs and learned several lessons in knowing joy in all three types of jobs.

CHAPTER 4 JOY IN TRANSITIONS

Jesus knew joy, because He prayed in transitions. We reviewed that transitions come in many forms: life, home, relationships, and jobs. Because of its broad applicability and inherent challenges, we focused on a specific job transition: unemployment.

Although Jesus Himself was never unemployed, He did go through a transition from His earthly ministry to enter heaven. There, His permanent priesthood continues, for He "always lives to intercede for [those who draw near to God through Him]" (Hebrews 7:25).

Jesus spoke frequently to His disciples about that transition. Jesus remained goal-oriented in His transition, undeterred by His enemies, especially Satan, who could do nothing to hold Him back.

From an action standpoint, we highlighted both Jesus' public and private prayers. His prayer time prepared Him for "go time": going to the cross. And this was where His saving work would be completed.

CHAPTER 5   JOY IN RELATIONSHIPS

Jesus knew joy, because He prayed in transitions. As Jesus journeyed towards the joy set before Him (Hebrews 12:2), His relationships were among His greatest joys and greatest trials. Whether it was friends or enemies who let Him down, Jesus consistently modeled a strong action: He forgave. In His first recorded words from the cross Jesus demonstrated true love through forgiveness, praying, "Father, forgive them, for they do not know what they are doing" (Luke 23:34 NIV).

In an act of love demonstrated at the cross, on the cross, and beyond the cross, Jesus forgave them! What a beautiful representation of love in action!

An important lesson we learned was that when we forgive others, especially those closest to us, we please God and impact His kingdom in unimaginable ways!

CHAPTER 6   JOY IN THE DEATH OF A LOVED ONE

Jesus knew joy, because He promised in the death of a loved one. Before noon on the first Good Friday, Jesus and two criminals were on full display before the onlookers assembled to witness His crucifixion. Here, in His second of seven recorded sayings on the cross, Jesus promised a repentant thief, whom Jesus loved (John 3:16), that glory awaited him: "Jesus answered him, 'Truly I tell you, today you will be with me in paradise.'" Luke 23:43 (NIV)

We discussed the "best of both worlds" approach to living for Christ now vs. waiting until just before you die, a day none of us wakes up knowing. In addition to the delicate approach to mourning with a loved one, we also considered how Jesus ministered to those who mourned Lazarus: Jesus wept.

Indeed, on our Journey to Joy, we, like Jesus, can experience joy even in the death of a loved one.

PART 3 JOY THROUGH INNER TRIALS

CHAPTER 7 JOY IN REJECTION

Jesus knew joy, because He planned for rejection. The cross stood as the brutal physical reality of the world rejecting Jesus. Yet despite the agony and pain the cross promised, Jesus' third recorded saying from the cross clearly demonstrates how He planned not only for His rejection but also for His mother. The apostle John, to whom Jesus entrusts His mother, records in John 19:26-27 (NASB), "When Jesus then saw His mother, and the disciple whom He loved standing nearby, He said to His mother, 'Woman, behold, your son!' Then He said to the disciple, 'Behold, your mother!' From that hour the disciple took her into his own household."

Jesus frequently encountered rejection Himself. In fact, since the earliest times humans have been rejecting God. We reviewed a number of historical examples.

Jesus had much to say about His own rejection, and ours. Because we follow Jesus, we will be rejected, so we should plan for it.

CHAPTER 8 JOY IN PAIN

Jesus knew joy, because He anguished in pain. Throughout His earthly ministry, Jesus encountered various kinds of pain, ranging from passive (public ridicule) to pronounced (the cross). And Jesus warned His disciples of His forthcoming trials, repeatedly explaining the pain He would experience at the hands of the Jewish leadership. Matthew records (16:21 NIV), "From that time on Jesus began to explain to his disciples that he must go to Jerusalem and suffer many things at the hands of the elders, the chief priests and the teachers of the law, and that he must be killed and on the third day be raised to life."

We marveled that Jesus often remained silent before His accusers and that He never complained. We also learned that God uses inhuman physical pain to work glorious results. Jesus talked about His pain and about His disciples' pain, anticipating that they will suffer for Him, too.

The pain Jesus endured brought about the greatest joy we can ever know.

CHAPTER 9 JOY IN SICKNESS

Jesus knew joy, because He thirsted in sickness. In His cry, we keenly sense Jesus' humanity. But while Jesus' broken body thirsted for water, His spiritual thirst to do His Father's will was far greater. Throughout His earthly walk Jesus encountered sick and thirsty people who desired to know the Messiah. *Not* knowing Jesus is far worse than any sickness: He went to the cross so that we could know Him. We saw three examples of sick and thirsty people He encountered.

We reviewed how Jesus ministered to thirsty people: the bleeding woman who thirsted for healing; the Samaritan woman at the well, "sick" from her lifestyle and thirsting for salvation; and a sick, beloved friend Lazarus and his family, who thirsted to understand why Jesus hadn't saved Lazarus.

In healing Lazarus, and thereby glorifying God, Jesus foreshadowed His own thirst and sickness of death on the cross, and His subsequent glorification, which the Father promised!

CHAPTER 10 JOY IN MISERY

Jesus knew joy, because He cried out in misery. Beyond the overwhelming agony of crucifixion, there was great joy in what was to come: Jesus completed His atoning work. He persevered through the most difficult trial and saw the joy of completing His race. After Jesus cried out in agony, He said, "It is finished" and "gave up his spirit" (John 19:30 NIV).

Jesus also experienced emotional misery as He mourned Jerusalem's refusal to obey God and as He predicted the dire judgement the Romans would inflict upon Jerusalem.

We learned that God allows trials to enter our lives, and these often involve misery. However, when we enter into misery with Christ, we can be assured we will ultimately leave misery behind, because Jesus Himself does not remain in misery. God will build valuable attributes in us, such as patience and perseverance, and we can be confident that we will pass through misery *with* Him, not alone.

PART 4   VICTORIOUS JOY!

CHAPTER 11   JOY IN DYING TO SELF

Jesus knew joy, because He died to self. Dying to self is the essence of the Christian life: taking up our cross and following Christ, as Jesus taught (Luke 9:24): "If anyone wants to come after me, let him deny himself, take up his cross daily, and follow me. For whoever wants to save his life will lose it, but whoever loses his life for my sake will save it."

In fact, Jesus says we *can't* be His disciples *without* following Him: "And if you do not carry your own cross and follow me, you cannot be my disciple" (Luke 14:27 NLT).

Jesus revealed His obedience to the Father as an act of dying to self through a torturous death on the cross (John 8:28-30). Jesus *always* does what pleases the Father. His action reflects this guide's main premise: **Joy is knowing Jesus, following Him through all our trials.**

Jesus' perfect example demonstrated that dying to self saved many lives, led to rejoicing, and elicited His cry on the cross, "Father, into your hands I commit my spirit."

CHAPTER 12   DESTINATION JOY?

Jesus knew joy, because He conquered death! In this chapter we saw the culmination of His journey to joy. The apostle Paul celebrates Christ's conquering death because He "will never die again. Death no longer has any power over him" (Romans 6:9 GWT).

The joy that so many thought had been extinguished by Jesus' death in fact brought new life for all who would follow Jesus in His suffering! The writer of Hebrews celebrated His victory in 12:2 (NIV): **"Let us fix our eyes on Jesus, the pioneer and perfecter of our faith, who for the joy set before Him endured the cross, scorning its shame, and sat down at the right hand of the throne of God."**

Yes, Jesus knew the cross's torment, shame, and death, but He also knew the joy set before Him by conquering death. Here is the glorious outcome: **Jesus' Journey to Joy is complete!**

CHAPTER 13 QUESTIONS:

1. Which chapter was most interesting to you? Why?
2. Which chapter was most convicting to you? Why?
3. What are some of the joys you've experienced in your Journey to Joy?
4. What are some of the challenges you've experienced in your Journey to Joy?
5. What are some ways you can know joy going forward in your life?

14

CONCLUSION

We began *A Family Guide to Joy* with a simple question: How can I know joy in all circumstances? And we examined the apostle James's teaching that pure joy can be ours at every station of life's journey. *"Consider it pure joy, my brothers and sisters, whenever you face trials of many kinds, because you know that the testing of your faith produces perseverance."* James 1:2-3 (NIV)

Throughout this guide, we repeatedly considered three journeys:

1. Jesus' Journey to Joy
2. My Journey to Joy
3. Your Journey to Joy

Though our journeys are measured in finite years, Jesus' Journey to Joy is complete and everlasting. Our journeys will converge with His in boundless eternity! *"Let us fix our eyes on Jesus, the pioneer and perfecter of our faith, who for the joy set before Him endured the cross, scorning its shame, and sat down at the right hand of the throne of God."* Hebrews 12:2 (NIV)

As we've seen through Jesus' Journey to Joy, joy in and from our circumstances may not come right away. You may be in the middle of "weeping…for a night" (Psalm 30:5), but that night does *not* last forever. Rejoicing comes in the morning! Joy comes because Jesus perseveres with us. And it comes because Jesus already walked this path, and He leads us in carrying our cross to complete our journey into His presence.

In closing, we still may ask, "So, why do we have to go through these trials?" But that's not the question really. The *real* question is why would we NOT want to go and persevere through these trials, knowing the joy Jesus will bring through them?

> **Joy is knowing Jesus, following Him through all our trials.**

CHAPTER 14 QUESTIONS:

1. How has God used this guide's Joy Challenges to grow you closer to Him and your family?
2. What's the most impactful lesson you learned? Why?
3. How ready are you ready to make the claim, "I can know joy in all circumstances?"
4. "Why would we NOT want to go and persevere through these trials, knowing the joy Jesus will bring through them?" Share your answer.
5. Who else needs this guide? Share a copy of this guide with three friends.

CHAPTERS 1 – 14
CHALLENGES AND QUESTIONS

CHAPTER 1

JOY CHALLENGE #1: What are you willing to sacrifice to know joy in your life?

CHAPTER 1 QUESTIONS:
1. What are you looking to get out of this study?
2. What are you looking to contribute to this study?
3. In your own words, how would you define joy?
4. What's stealing your joy right now?
5. How did Jesus model joy?
6. How does knowing Jesus help us walk joyfully in our faith?

CHAPTER 2

JOY CHALLENGE #2: Explain how you can know joy in good times.

CHAPTER 2 QUESTIONS:
1. Knowing God is the source of all joy, how does that change your outlook?
2. Why does Jesus seem most joyous when we turn from death to life?
3. Which lesson was most helpful to you? Why?
4. How can a good time become a trial?
5. Why are good times without God not good times at all?
6. What's your life's best moment? Why?

CHAPTER 3

JOY CHALLENGE #3: Describe how you can know joy in your daily work.

CHAPTER 3 QUESTIONS:
1. Why is our work of supreme importance to God?
2. How well do you balance your work time and your quiet times with God? How can you improve this?
3. What's the greatest job you've had? Most miserable job you've had? Why?
4. How did God bring joy through these jobs?
5. Which lesson was most helpful to you? Why?
6. List three things God is teaching you in your daily work.

CHAPTER 4

JOY CHALLENGE #4: Articulate how you can know joy in transitions.

CHAPTER 4 QUESTIONS:
1. Our transitions on earth – employed or unemployed – are in light of the cross. Jesus modeled transitions for us. How so?
2. Jesus prayed through His transition. How can prayer help us through our transitions?
3. Which lesson was most helpful to you? Why?
4. Why does unemployment carry such a stigma even though so many have been unemployed?
5. Does unemployment indicate failure or success? Why?
6. How can you minister to someone who's in transition right now?

CHAPTER 5

JOY CHALLENGE #5: Consider how you can know joy through your most broken relationship.

CHAPTER 5 QUESTIONS:
1. Why are relationships so important to God? To us?
2. How has forgiveness impacted your relationships?
3. Jesus forgave His enemies, so how can we forgive our enemies?
4. Who in your life do you need to forgive?
5. Do you sense that your most broken relationship is with Jesus? If not, what's your most broken relationship?

6. Explain in 30 seconds, how did it get so broken? What can you do to help repair it?
7. Which lesson was most helpful to you? Why?

CHAPTER 6

JOY CHALLENGE #6: Reflect on how you can know joy in the death of a loved one.

CHAPTER 6 QUESTIONS:
1. Why is the "best of both worlds" approach (live for myself now, choose Christ just before I die) naive?
2. In light of Jesus' promise of eternal life, how does that affect the way you live your life now?
3. Jesus models for us that we, too, often must pass through deepest sorrow to get to joy. What examples can you share from your own life?
4. "At Calvary, Satan thought he was winning…until he lost!" How so?
5. Which lesson was most helpful to you? Why?
6. How can you comfort someone who has suffered the death of a loved one?

CHAPTER 7

JOY CHALLENGE #7: Discover how you can know joy in rejection.

CHAPTER 7 QUESTIONS:
1. Why did Jesus allow Himself to be rejected?
2. Why have humans continued to reject God?
3. What did Jesus say about the world rejecting His followers? What are some examples of this?
4. Why is rejection so hard for us to take?
5. Which lesson was most helpful to you? Why?
6. How can you bring joy to someone who's facing rejection?

CHAPTER 8

JOY CHALLENGE #8: Share how you can know joy in pain.

CHAPTER 8 QUESTIONS:
1. What did Jesus say about His pain?
2. What did Jesus say about His disciples' pain?
3. What's the most pain you've experienced? How did you handle it?
4. Which lesson was most helpful to you? Why?
5. What lessons did God teach you through your pain?
6. How can you bring joy to someone who's suffering in pain?

CHAPTER 9

JOY CHALLENGE #9: Talk about how you can know joy in sickness.

CHAPTER 9 QUESTIONS:
1. What's the longest you've ever been sick? Briefly, how did you get so sick?
2. How can we "rejoice with Him in times God heals us, but trust Him in times He doesn't"?
3. Many Samaritans believed in Jesus because of the testimony of the woman at the well. How can you share your testimony of the Living Water? With whom can you share it?
4. Which lesson was most helpful to you? Why?
5. How can you know joy when someone you love experiences sickness?
6. How can you bring joy to someone who's suffering now in sickness?

CHAPTER 10

JOY CHALLENGE #10: Expand on how you can know joy by crying out in misery.

CHAPTER 10 QUESTIONS:
1. Why was Jesus willing to endure the misery of the cross?
2. "Misery is a tool God uses to make us more like Him." How so?
3. To what degree has misery been a part of your trials?
4. Why do we blame God when we find ourselves in trials?
5. Which lesson was most helpful to you? Why?
6. How can you minister to someone who's experiencing misery?

CHAPTER 11

JOY CHALLENGE #11: Choose one way you can die to self and how you'll go about it.

CHAPTER 11 QUESTIONS:
1. What did Jesus accomplish in dying on the cross? Why did He do that?
2. What does Jesus mean in Luke 14:27 that we cannot be His disciples if we don't carry our cross and follow Him?
3. Why is it so hard to die to self?
4. What's one thing you've sensed the Holy Spirit nudge you to do in order to die to self? Did you obey? What were the results?
5. How easy or difficult is it to challenge someone to die to self? How would you go about it?
6. Which lesson was most helpful to you? Why?

CHAPTER 12

JOY CHALLENGE #12: How can *you* know joy in all circumstances? Share your answer with a friend.

CHAPTER 12 QUESTIONS:
1. How does knowing that Jesus' Journey to Joy is complete encourage you in your Journey to Joy?
2. Why was it so significant that Jesus first appeared to Mary Magdalene?
3. Why does death have no power over those who follow Christ?
4. Which lesson was most helpful to you? Why?
5. Why will we not reach destination joy here on earth?
6. Knowing what you know, are you willing to allow God to conquer YOUR biggest fears? How so?

CHAPTER 13

CHAPTER 13 QUESTIONS:
1. Which chapter was most interesting to you? Why?
2. Which chapter was most convicting to you? Why?

3. What are some of the joys you've experienced in your Journey to Joy?
4. What are some of the challenges you've experienced in your Journey to Joy?
5. What are some ways you can know joy going forward in your life?

CHAPTER 14

CHAPTER 14 QUESTIONS:

1. How has God used this Guide's Joy Challenges to grow you closer to Him and your family?
2. What's the most impactful lesson you learned? Why?
3. How ready are you ready to make the claim, "I can know joy in all circumstances?"
4. "Why would we NOT want to go and persevere through these trials, knowing the joy Jesus will bring through them?" Share your answer.
5. Who else needs this guide? Share a copy of this guide with three friends.

AFTERWORD

This letter from Denny needs little explanation, but it highlights how picking up our cross and following Jesus' Journey to Joy can change our lives forever. Only God can do that! Without changing Denny's circumstances, God changed Denny's life forever, and He can change your life forever, too!

Until I met a man named Travis Zimmerman and heard his story, Job was the only man of God I could relate to. "For sighing has become my daily food; My groans pour out like water. What I feared has come upon me; what I dreaded has happened to me. I have no peace, no quietness; I have no rest, but only turmoil." Job 3:24-26 (NIV)

I kept telling myself that God's ways are higher than my ways, yet I found myself asking: why? Why my health, my family's health, my career coming to a screeching halt, my home in foreclosure and for pity's sake: why my marriage, why now? Is this not the "for better or worse" that we both vowed to love each other through? Why does she still need closure from her abusive past? Why have we so recklessly learned to abuse each other now in so many ways? How could God be doing this to me?

I quietly wondered what Jeremiah asks best: "Why do the faithless live at ease?" (Jeremiah 12:1). Yet, you know me, Lord; you see me and test my thoughts about you.

Having completely given up on ever discovering rhyme or reason for my torture, I found God's answer by divine appointment. Shortly after I stopped calling myself Job and began picking up the pieces of my brokenness, I met a man named Travis Zimmerman at a men's conference. His story has forever changed the way I think. While none of the actual circumstances in my life have changed, it is my perspective along with the faith of a mustard seed which moved a mountain for me.

Travis reportedly wasn't even going to read from his blog from August 31st entitled "How God Conquered My Biggest Fear," but for some reason the Holy Spirit led him to share. I'm certain that reason was me.

I will be forever grateful for that day! After hearing a man of God whose pain mirrored my own and whose brokenness was at a depth that someone at rock bottom could relate to, it was by divine appointment that these words penetrated my hardening heart:

"Over this past decade, I guided you through all of your life's biggest fears to show you that you can always trust Me."

It was only then that I realized that God didn't do that TO me but FOR me. It's been 6 months or so since the conference, yet the enlightenment still overwhelms me with joy. Yes, JOY! I know I may not be out of the valley, but I will move on with my life, fearing no evil because I finally realized God is with me.

Most grateful salutations,

Denny
February 2018

ACKNOWLEDGMENTS

Jesus, I love You with all my heart!

I love my bride, Suzanne, to whom I have been joyfully married for nearly 24 years now. I can't imagine life without you, and I have such joy in knowing God has brought us together and taught us so many lessons about loving Him and others.

With my bride, I rejoice in our five wonderful children who bring such joy to our lives: Elizabeth Mae; Koen Irwin; Treyton David; Grantham Everett; and Braden Christian. I thank God for the joy of being your dad!

A Faithful Dad's board members are wonderful servants of the Most High God: Pastor Dave Biser; Yolie DeShong; Dan Gobat; Andrew Golembiesky; Carl Reeder; Cody Wells; and my bride, Suzanne Zimmerman. Your encouragement, guidance, accountability, and love for Christ propel us to joyfully and obediently walk in faith on the path that God has called us.

A very special thank you to my editors, Professor Annie Schreiber and Lance Clark, my interior layout consultant, Matthew Elliott, my project artist, Trey Zimmerman, and my proofreader, Gail Eckenroad. Your graciousness, tact, and direction were a gift from God Himself – thank you!

God, following Your call on my life has been the most joyful experience of my life: "Travis, speak My Word, and I will take care of the rest...." In You, Jesus, there is boundless joy!

NOTES

PART 1
C. S. Lewis, *The Weight of Glory, and Other Addresses* (New York, HarperCollins, 1949).

CHAPTER 1
Oswald J. Smith, "There is joy in serving Jesus," released 1931, Hall-Mack Company.

Karl Barth Quotes. BrainyQuote.com, Xplore Inc, 2018. https://www.brainyquote.com/quotes/karl_barth_380251, accessed May 1, 2018.

C. Davis, "Joy," in *Evangelical Dictionary of Theology, Second Edition*, edited by Walter A. Elwell, 636. Grand Rapids, Baker Books, 2001.

Life Application Study Bible, New International Version, 1556. Grand Rapids, Tyndale House Publishers, 2005.

Life Application Study Bible, New International Version, 35. Grand Rapids, Tyndale House Publishers, 2005.

Johnny Nash, "I Can See Clearly Now," released June 23, 1972, Epic Records.

"The Key to the Christian's Joy," Ligonier Ministries, accessed May 1, 2018, https://www.ligonier.org/blog/key-christians-joy/.

William MacDonald, "Romans," in *The Believer's Bible Commentary*, edited by Art Farstad, 1707. Nashville, Thomas Nelson Books, 1989.

RV State Sticker Trailer Map USA States Visited Decal Wall Motorhome, Suny-Stores, accessed May 1, 2018, https://ebay.to/2w1apER.

CHAPTER 2

Ray Gilbert, "Zip-a-Dee-Doo-Dah," released 1946, Walt Disney Music Company.

"10.1. The Jewish Wedding Analogy," Bible Study Tools, accessed May 1, 2018, https://www.biblestudytools.com/commentaries/revelation/related-topics/the-jewish-wedding-analogy.html.

"Gill's exposition of Genesis 1:31," The Bible Hub, accessed May 1, 2018, http://biblehub.com/genesis/1-31.htm.

PART 2

A Christmas Story, MGM, 1983.

CHAPTER 3

William Shakespeare, *As You Like It*, act 1, sc 3, L11 (1599).

Evangelical Convictions: A Theological Exposition of the Statement of Faith of the Evangelical Free Church of America (Minneapolis, Free Church Press, 2011), 112.

Lunch atop a Skyscraper (Branded Entertainment Network)

Phil Spector, Barry Mann, Cynthia Weil, "You've Lost That Lovin' Feeling," released November, 1964, Philles Records.

CHAPTER 4

Harry S. Truman Quotes. BrainyQuote.com, Xplore Inc, 2018. https://www.brainyquote.com/quotes/harry_s_truman_132381, accessed May 1, 2018.

"The Very Worst Thing That Could Happen When You Lose Your Job," MensHealth.com. https://www.menshealth.com/health/a19533897/unemployment-suicide-risk/, accessed May 1, 2018.

CHAPTER 5

Mother Teresa Quotes. BrainyQuote.com, Xplore Inc, 2018.
https://www.brainyquote.com/quotes/mother_teresa_108724,
accessed May 1, 2018.

CHAPTER 6

Billy Graham Quotes. BrainyQuote.com, Xplore Inc, 2018.
https://www.brainyquote.com/quotes/billy_graham_383577, accessed
May 1, 2018.

PART 3

Life Application Study Bible, New International Version, Preamble. Grand
Rapids, Tyndale House Publishers, 2005.

CHAPTER 7

Rodney Dangerfield Quotes. AZQuotes.com, 2018.
http://www.azquotes.com/quote/626206, accessed May 1, 2018.

CHAPTER 8

"Anguish," Google Dictionary, https://bit.ly/2Fx5IlN, accessed May
1, 2018.

"A Physician's View of the Crucifixion of Jesus Christ," CBN.
http://www1.cbn.com/medical-view-of-the-crucifixion-of-jesus-christ,
accessed May 1, 2018.

"For Caviezel, playing Christ proved to be a challenge," Today.
https://www.today.com/popculture/caviezel-playing-christ-proved-
be-challenge-wbna4297029, accessed May 1, 2018.

William MacDonald, "The Gospel According to Matthew," in *The
Believer's Bible Commentary*, edited by Art Farstad, 1239. Nashville,
Thomas Nelson Books, 1989.

CHAPTER 9

Thomas Fuller Quotes. BrainyQuote.com, Xplore Inc, 2018.
https://www.brainyquote.com/quotes/thomas_fuller_380713,
accessed May 1, 2018.

"A Physician's View of the Crucifixion of Jesus Christ," CBN.
http://www1.cbn.com/medical-view-of-the-crucifixion-of-jesus-christ,
accessed May 1, 2018.

CHAPTER 10

Philip Yancey Quotes. AZQuotes.com, 2018.
http://www.azquotes.com/quote/577624, accessed May 1, 2018.

"Misery," Google Dictionary, https://bit.ly/2Fx5IlN, accessed May 1,
2018.

"A Physician's View of the Crucifixion of Jesus Christ," CBN.
http://www1.cbn.com/medical-view-of-the-crucifixion-of-jesus-christ,
accessed May 1, 2018.

Flavius Josephus, *The Wars of the Jews or History of the Destruction of
Jerusalem*. https://www.gutenberg.org/files/2850/2850-h/2850-h.htm,
accessed May 1, 2018.

"Siege of Jerusalem (70 CE)," accessed May 1, 2018,
https://en.wikipedia.org/wiki/Siege_of_Jerusalem_(70_CE).

PART 4

Alfred H. Ackley, "I serve a Risen Savior," released 1933, Word Music.

CHAPTER 11

*Evangelical Convictions: A Theological Exposition of the Statement of Faith of the
Evangelical Free Church of America* (Minneapolis, Free Church Press,
2011), 112.

"Second Fiddle – From His Heart – Week of July 31,"
Christianity.com. https://www.christianity.com/devotionals/from-
his-heart-jeff-schreve/second-fiddle-from-his-heart-week-of-july-
31.html, accessed May 1, 2018.

William MacDonald, "The Gospel According to John," in *The Believer's
Bible Commentary*, edited by Art Farstad, 1525. Nashville, Thomas
Nelson Books, 1989.
Gary M. Burge, "John," in *Baker's Commentary on the Bible based on the
NIV*, edited by Walter A. Elwell, 865. Grand Rapids, Baker Books,
1989.

Life Application Study Bible, New International Version, 1768. Grand
Rapids, Tyndale House Publishers, 2005.

"A Physician's View of the Crucifixion of Jesus Christ," CBN.
http://www1.cbn.com/medical-view-of-the-crucifixion-of-jesus-christ,
accessed May 1, 2018.

"The Sayings of Jesus on the cross," accessed May 1, 2018,
https://en.wikipedia.org/wiki/Sayings_of_Jesus_on_the_cross.

Ibid.

CHAPTER 12

Jeremy Riddle, "Christ is Risen," released March 3, 2009, Vineyard
Worship.

"Woman," *International Standard Bible Encyclopedia, Volume 4* (Grand
Rapids, Wm. B. Eerdmans Publishing Company), 1094.

"What is the concept of 'already but not yet?'" GotQuestions.org.
https://www.gotquestions.org/already-not-yet.html, accessed May 1,
2018.

Mercy Me, "I can only imagine," released 1999, INO.

CHAPTER 13

"60 Quotes About Adversity," ChristianQuotes.info.
https://www.christianquotes.info/quotes-by-topic/quotes-about-adversity/#axzz5EHm1NtJc, accessed May 1, 2018.

C. Davis, "Joy," in *Evangelical Dictionary of Theology, Second Edition*, edited by Walter A. Elwell, 636. Grand Rapids, Baker Books, 2001.

INDEX OF SCRIPTURE REFERENCES

AKJV *Authorized King James Version*
Cambridge: Cambridge University Press (1611)

AMP *Amplified Bible*
La Habra, CA: The Lockman Foundation (2015)

BSB *Berean Study Bible*
Glassport, PA: Berean Bible (2016)

CEV *Contemporary English Version*
New York, NY: American Bible Society (1995)

ERV *Easy-to-Read Version*
Crete, IL: World Bible Translation Center (2004

ESV *English Standard Version*
Wheaton, IL: Good News Publishers (2011)

GWT *God's Word Translation*
Grand Rapids, MI: World Publishing, Inc. (1995)

HCSB *Holman Christian Study Bible*
Nashville, TN: Holman Bible Publishers (2009)

ICB *International Children's Bible*
Nashville, TN: Thomas Nelson, Inc. (1989)

ISV *International Standard Version*
Bellflower, CA: ISV Foundation (1996)

LEB *Lexham English Bible*
Bellingham, WA: Logos Bible Software (2012)

NASB *New American Standard Bible*
Anaheim, CA: Foundation Press (1973)

NET NET Bible
Garland, TX (1994)

NHEB *New Heart English Bible*
Public Domain Bibles (2010)

NIRV *New International Reader's Version*
Colorado Springs, CO: Biblica (2014)

NIV *New International Version*
Colorado Springs, CO: Biblica (1978, 1984, 2011)

NIVUK *New International Version – UK*
Colorado Springs, CO: Biblica (2011)

NLT *New Living Translation*
Wheaton, IL: Tyndale House Publishers (1996)

NOG *Names of God Bible*
Grand Rapids, MI: Baker Publishing Group (2011)

NRSV *New Revised Standard Edition*
New York, NY: National Council of Churches in Christ (1991)

PHILLIPS *J.B. Phillips New Testament*
Archbishop's Council of the Church of England (1972)

TLB *The Living Bible*
Wheaton, IL: Tyndale House Publishers (1979)

TLV *Tree of Life Version*
Grand Rapids, MI: Baker Publishing Group (2015)

CHAPTER 1

1. James 1:2-3 (NIV)
2. Matthew 11:28-30 (NIV)
3. John 17:3 (BSB)
4. John 13:13
5. Acts 5:41 (NLT)
6. John 13:7 (NIV)
7. Revelation 6:10 (BSB)
8. Romans 8:28
9. Luke 9:23 (CSB)
10. Galatians 5:22
11. Proverbs 10:28 (CSB)
12. James 1:2-4
13. John 16:33 (NIV)
14. Philippians 4:4
15. Luke 24:26 (HCSB)
16. Hebrews 12:2 (NIV)
17. Galatians 1:4

CHAPTER 2

1. John 2:1-2 (AMP)
2. John 2:10-11 (NIV)
3. Matthew 14:13-21
4. John 9:25
5. Genesis 1:4
6. Genesis 1:8
7. Genesis 1:12
8. Genesis 1:18
9. Genesis 1:21
10. Genesis 1:25
11. Genesis 1:31 (NLT)
12. Matthew 3:16-17 (CEV)
13. 1 Chronicles 16:27 (ESV)
14. Revelation 21:23 (WEB)
15. Luke 15:4-7 (NIV)
16. Luke 15:8-10 (PHILLIPS)
17. Luke 15:21-24 (NOG)

18. Acts 3:15
19. Hebrews 12:2
20. Ecclesiastes 7:14 (NIV)
21. Deuteronomy 8:10-14 (HCSB)
22. Deuteronomy 8:15-17 (NLV)
23. Deuteronomy 8:18-20 (NET)

CHAPTER 3

1. John 4:34 (NIV)
2. Matthew 13:55 (WEB)
3. Mark 6:3 (GWT)
4. Colossians 3:23-24
5. Isaiah 61:7 (ISV)
6. Hebrews 10:5-7 (NIV)
7. Mark 4:13 (NIV)
8. Matthew 15:16 (NIV)
9. Mark 3:1-6 (NRSV)
10. Mark 1:35 (CEV)
11. Luke 5:16 (CSB)
12. John 4:34-38 (NIV)
13. John 3:16-17 (ESV)
14. Ecclesiastes 2:24 (NLT)
15. Romans 15:13 (ESV)
16. Genesis 3:17 (AKJV)
17. Psalm 16:5-6 (HCSB)
18. Philippians 2:14 (BSB)
19. 1 Timothy 6:10 (NKJV)
20. Jeremiah 38:6 (NIV)
21. Genesis 31:40-41 (TLV)
22. 1 Samuel 19:10 (NIV)
23. Psalm 95:1-5 (AMP)

CHAPTER 4

1. Luke 22:41-42 (NIV)
2. Matthew 16:21 (BSB)
3. Luke 13:32 (NIV)
4. 1 John 2:2

5. John 14:28-31 (NIV)
6. Hebrews 7:25 (BSB)
7. John 17:4 (NLT)
8. Luke 22:39-40 (TPT)
9. Luke 22:41-44 (NIV)
10. Matthew 25:45-46 (NLT)
11. Philippians 4:12 (CEV)

CHAPTER 5

1. Luke 23:34 (NIV)
2. James 1:9
3. Hebrews 12:2
4. Matthew 6:14-15 (ERV)
5. Matthew 5:11-12 (NET)
6. Matthew 23:13 (NASB)
7. John 11:53 (WNT)
8. Mark 1:15 (NIRV)
9. John 10:31-33 (NLT)
10. Matthew 5:43-45 (NASB)
11. Luke 23:34 (NIV)
12. Matthew 26:31-34 (NTE)
13. Luke 22:60-62 (ISV)
14. John 21:15-17 (NIV)
15. Acts 2:41
16. 2 Corinthians 5:21 (NLT)
17. Matthew 26:27-28 (ESV)
18. 1 John 4:10 (NIV)
19. Psalm 23
20. John 8:10-11
21. Psalm 23:1-6 (KJV)

CHAPTER 6

1. John 11:35 (NIV)
2. John 3:16
3. Luke 23:28-43 (NIV)
4. John 11:33-35 (NASB)
5. John 11:35

6. John 11:36 (CSB)
7. Ezekiel 18:32 (NET)
8. 2 Peter 3:9 (NIV)
9. Mark 10:43-44 (NIV)
10. 1 Corinthians 55,57 (NIV)

CHAPTER 7

1. John 19:26-27 (NASB)
2. Genesis 2:8
3. Genesis 1:28 (NCV)
4. Genesis 2:17 (CSB)
5. Genesis 3:6 (TLB)
6. Genesis 3:14
7. Genesis 3:17
8. Numbers 11:18-20 (NIV)
9. Samuel 8:6-7 (NIV)
10. Isaiah 53:3 (NLT)
11. Isaiah 53:11 (NLT)
12. 1 John 4:19 (WEB)
13. 1 John 1:9-11 (ESV)
14. John 1:11 (NLT)
15. Luke 9:28-29 (NIV)
16. Mark 12:10 (CSB)
17. Luke 9:22 (ISV)
18. Luke 17:25 (HCSB)
19. Matthew 8:34 (EHV)
20. Mark 6:3 (NLT)
21. John 12:12-13 (NRSV)
22. Luke 23:18 (CEV)
23. Matthew 27:41-42 (AMP)
24. John 15:18-19 (GW)
25. Acts 5:40-41 (NIV)
26. Matthew 10:22 (TLV)
27. James 1:2 (NIV)
28. John 12:38 (LEB)

CHAPTER 8

1. Matthew 27:46 (NIV)
2. Isaiah 53:3 (NIV)
3. Psalm 22:14 (KJV)
4. Matthew 16:21 (NIV)
5. Matthew 25:52-63 (NIRV)
6. Mark 14:64-65 (NIVUK)
7. Isaiah 53:7 (CSB)
8. Philippians 2:14-15
9. John 19:1 (NIV)
10. John 19:1-3 (BSB)
11. John 19:14-16 (NIV)
12. Matthew 27:46 (NIV)
13. Galatians 3:13
14. Matthew 10:17-25
15. Mathew 10:17-18 (NET)
16. Psalm 89:26
17. Psalm 126:1-6 (BSB)

CHAPTER 9

1. John 19:28 (NIV)
2. Mark 5:24-29 (NIVUK)
3. Mark 5:34 (NIV)
4. Mark 5:29 (NIVUK)
5. John 4:9-14 (ICB)
6. John 4:39 (ESV)
7. Matthew 9:35 (HCSB)
8. John 11:21 (NLT)
9. John 11:4 (NLT)
10. John 12:27-28 (NASB)
11. Philippians 4:7
12. Psalm 138:1-8 (NLT)

CHAPTER 10

1. John 19:30 (NIV)
2. Luke 13:34 (ESV)

6. John 20:11-18 (NIV)
7. John 10:3 (NIV)
8. Matthew 14:21
9. Matthew 15:38
10. John 20:19-20 (NIV)
11. Mark 13:26 (BSB)
12. Revelation 21:3-4 (ERV)
13. 1 Peter 4:19 (NIV)
14. James 1:2-3 (NIV)
15. Luke 17:20-21 (NIV)
16. Hebrews 12:2
17. John 14:16 (NASB)
18. Galatians 5:25 (BSB)
19. Romans 5:3-5 (BSB)
20. 1 Peter 1:3-4 (NIV)
21. 1 Peter 1:8-9 (NIV)
22. James 1:12 (NIV)
23. James 1:2-3 (NIV)
24. Psalm 84:10 (HCSB)

PART 5
1. Philippians 1:9-11 (NIV)

CHAPTER 13

1. James 1:2-3 (NIV)

A Faithful Dad's Guide to Legacy

What legacy do I want to leave for my family?

This is arguably one of the most, if not the most, critical question a dad - regardless of age - will ever answer. Yet, as we think through it, a legacy isn't just something that you produce at the end of your life, something you just whip up quickly in the kitchen like some microwave leftovers for your kids to gobble down after soccer practice.

No, a legacy is, of course, something that is built up – or torn down – over time, a lifetime to be specific. It's something developed day by day, interaction by interaction with those we love, those who love us, those closest to us. So, when I'm gone from this earth, what will I be remembered for, both good…and bad?

Through authentic experiences and biblical examples, *A Faithful Dad's Guide to Legacy* will equip you to leave a lasting legacy your family will treasure.

A FAITHFUL DAD

Tagline: A faithful dad in every home.

Vision: Follow Jesus. Lead your family. Leave a legacy.
(1 Corinthians 11:1)

Mission: We encourage dads and families. (2 Peter 1:3)

Core Values:

- We encourage dads to wholeheartedly follow Jesus.
(Matthew 4:19-20)
- We affirm the importance of marriage in transforming families.
(Genesis 2:24)
- We believe dads instill their faith into their children.
(Deuteronomy 6:4-9)
- We inspire dads to pass along a lasting legacy to their families.
(1 Corinthians 3:10-15)
- We motivate dads to build godly friendships in the brotherhood of
Christ. (Proverbs 27:17)
- We strive with dads to achieve a healthy life balance.
(Ecclesiastes 3:1)
- We desire thankfulness and reconciliation between every man and
his dad. (Exodus 20:12)

Made in the USA
Middletown, DE
13 February 2020

84167522R10119